Food & Flowers
for the Four Seasons

Food & Flowers
for the Four Seasons

JOHN TOVEY and DEREK BRIDGES

MACDONALD & CO
London & Sydney

To Pat and Sara,
for their encouragement
D.B.

A MACDONALD BOOK

© John Tovey, Derek Bridges, Susan Fleming 1983
First published in Great Britain 1983
by Macdonald & Co (Publishers) Ltd
London & Sydney

Photographs by Peter Smith,
© Macdonald & Co (Publishers) Ltd
Illustration on page 69 by Janet Good
Designed by Richard Johnson
Seasonal spread illustrations by Maggie Raynor

ISBN 0 356 07878 7

Reproduced, printed and bound in Great Britain by
Hazell Watson & Viney Limited,
Member of the BPCC Group,
Aylesbury, Bucks

Macdonald & Co (Publishers) Ltd
Maxwell House
74 Worship Street
London EC2A 2EN
A BPCC plc Company

Contents

Food, Cooking and Party Drinks

There was a time when seasonal cooking was very much regimented, when food grew by the laws of Mother Nature and God alone. Nowadays, with the advent of sophisticated farming and preserving methods, and the speedy transportation of goods of all kinds from all ends of the Earth, we can cook and eat virtually anything we like at any time of the year. Salads, once the province of summer only, can be eaten all year round, as can strawberries; imported apples keep the doctor away daily, instead of just in autumn; and Kenyan French beans and *mange-tout* flood the markets up and down the country.

Undeniably this bounty is appreciated, but I liked the seasonal 'discipline', with the anticipation of each season's particular and individual tastes: frozen lamb can't compare with local spring lamb; strawberries all year round are boring, and don't taste the same; game *is* best in autumn, because fresh; newly picked fruit is infinitely tastier than frozen or imported; and vegetables straight from the garden, still with a bit of muck on them, are superior to even the finest imported wares. Give me a local tomato plucked from the plant any day in preference to the Italian or Spanish one, however large and beautiful.

With these admittedly personal strictures in mind, I have given seasonal menus that include the best of the traditional seasonal fare. With my food for different types of party each season, and Derek's ideas for decorating your house for those parties, I hope you have a wonderfully successful entertaining year.

Party Drinks

I very rarely drink anything but wine – but I must admit the occasional rum toddy, a gin and tonic at lunchtime, and my favourite Sunday Bloody Mary, are delicious.

I am continually being asked what should be drunk with what, or what wine is a particularly good buy. Some people actually anticipate their question with the phrase 'You're an expert on wine' – at which I cringe with true humility and quite honestly reply 'I'm *not* an expert, but I do know what I like.'

And that's the first thing for me: it's not a fine palate or a full purse, but a high degree of truth to yourself. If you sip a recommended wine that you personally think is a load of rubbish, don't go on about how awful you think it is, don't falsely praise it, just discreetly get rid of it – but *not* in the flower arrangement, which would be bad for Derek's blood pressure as well as the flowers!

I always try a new wine by gently twirling the contents round so they just lap up the sides of the glass (if the wine clings it is a sign of body), and then having a good old sniff! Sweet fruity. Dry gooseberry. Diesel fuel. Blackcurrants. Rich fruit. I take some into my mouth, and swill it around a little with lips slightly open. This is a funny sensation at first, but does release the flavour and bouquet on to your palate. Wine experts are dab hands at spitting out into the spittoon, but I don't sample in sufficient quantities to warrant this. I let the first mouthful slowly dribble down my throat and hit my belly.

If you like the wine after tasting it as above, make copious notes as to why, and then perhaps buy a couple of bottles. If you still like it after drinking those, go to town and buy a case.

I love French wines, but I've had some that were quite ghastly, so more and more when entertaining, I tend to serve wines from South Africa (and I have a full South African wine list at Miller Howe). These are readily available from two constant sources of supply (Collisons at 7 Bury Street, London SW1, and the Cape Wine Centre at 46 Great Marlborough Street, London W1). The stringent regulations on vine growing and wine producing in South Africa have meant one very rarely finds a poor or indifferent wine (although it's seldom that one encounters a truly great one). The mistake that people initially make is to compare the wine to one they like that is produced in the northern hemisphere. Time after time I've heard people say, 'Yes, an interesting wine, but not like the French'; how can it be when the soil, climate and extremes are so totally different?

For very special occasions, like a wedding, I know the norm is to serve champagne, but it's so expensive that if you're not too careful it can drain away all the pennies and pounds. You could serve sherry, a sparkling white wine, your favourite red or white for the meal, or you could try fortified wines. They're not especial favourites of mine, but sometimes they're delicious. At a spring wedding reception, for instance, the weather could still be cool, so a chilled white aperitif wine might tempt the guests to imbibe more than usual in order to get a warm glow inside. If you greet your guests with Madeira, you not only warm them up, but also give them something to talk about (it's not drunk as often as it should be).

There are four types of Madeira. Sercial is light, slightly sharp but fragrant, the driest of the four and is, in my opinion, the better for being served slightly chilled. Verdelhe is less dry, and is usually a soft wine with a smoked honey flavour to it. Bual is supposed to be a dessert wine, but there is no reason whatsoever why it shouldn't be drunk as an aperitif (it's very similar to Bristol Milk Sherry). Malmsey is the sweetest Madeira, but on a cold day, it can really bring on a glow. Wine experts will now give me the thumbs down, but a piece of orange skin the size of your fingernail in the Malmsey or Bual glasses is delightful; likewise lemon rind or a pimento stuffed olive in the drier wines.

Flowers and Flower Arranging

Every new book on flower arranging must demonstrate a fresh expression and creativeness, and this book does just that, with its linking together of food and flowers, and its emphasis on decorating your home for those special occasions when you entertain.

I must say straightaway that in no way do I wish to dictate what is right or what is wrong, or how you should decorate your home. A flower arrangement has infinite potential for variation: it can be as simple as a basket of daisies, as traditional as a silver bowl and red carnations, or as elaborate as you like. What I will do is to give you ideas that I like and that have worked for me, which you can adopt, adapt and possibly improve, to make them your own.

There are no set rules about decorating your home for entertaining. Don't forget the prime reason for the occasion: you want to entertain your guests in your home, you want them to enjoy themselves — as do you! From the moment you open the door, there should be a welcoming atmosphere, welcoming lights and warmth, delicious smells from the kitchen and — of course — lots of flowers. Plants and flowers, more than anything else, add life, colour and homeliness to a room. And so I hope you will enjoy the flowers and the ideas as you read your way through your four seasons of flower arranging.

Basic Equipment
You will probably already possess the basic equipment required for flower arranging — apart from the flowers themselves — scissors, secateurs and a sharp knife. In addition to the containers in which you will arrange your flowers, you will need florists' wires of all kinds — stub, reel and silver — floral foam, dri-foam, pin holders, and floral foam tape. As you get into the swing of things you will add to these other useful items, such as plasticine, drawing pins, wooden cocktail sticks and skewers, etc. Anything and everything — if it does a useful job — can have a place in the flower arranger's equipment.

Mechanics
A flower arrangement should look finished, easy, graceful and effortless — and should never give any hint of the behind-the-scene mechanics which have created such beauty. Every flower arranger needs to know and learn the general rules of mechanics: how to fasten a pin holder into a container, how to make practical holders for unusually shaped containers, how to soak floral foam, and how to properly anchor candles, fruit and other

different decorative items. Every so often a difficulty specific to a particular arrangement will arise – when the rules won't help – and you'll have to be inventive; you will discover, perhaps, that you can combine several methods to solve the problem, or you'll work out a much better method than any of the traditional ones. However, do make sure that your basic foundation is strong and good before going to the final stages of arrangement: we have all experienced the exasperation of a lovely arrangement falling over just as it's completed; when you start again that frustration will reveal itself in the actual arrangement. But if you do have any unusual ideas you are anxious to try out, don't be afraid to go ahead and do so.

Understanding basic mechanics does more than anything else to boost the flower arranger's self-confidence, the warm assurance that whatever your idea, you will be able to carry it out. Taking time to master these basic techniques, to acquire the basic habits of good craftsmanship, will save time in the long run.

Pinholders *I don't use pinholders often in my arrangements, but they are very useful. They come in all shapes and sizes, and are valuable for use in shallow containers. They must be fixed properly, and I use a good grade of modelling plasticine. You can buy this from floral sundries shops, art supply shops, gift and toy shops, and stationers, and can use it over and over again (the best types are less expensive in the long run, as the cheaper brands harden and crumble away after a while). After use, dry the plasticine off and allow it to dry thoroughly before using again.*

Both containers and pinholder must be absolutely dry. Work the plasticine in warm hands to make it pliable, and roll into a sausage shape. Press this sausage onto the outside lower edge of the pinholder's metal base, making a ring (or whatever shape the pinholder is). Turn the holder over and press it down onto the clean dry surface of the container, turn it slightly to make it adhere more firmly, and press it down, from the sides and top, and from the sides of the container. Now water can be put into the container without the pinholder coming adrift.

Floral Foam *Floral foam – a name to encompass many different commercial products – is a water-retaining plastic foam, which I find invaluable, and I use it much more than more old-fashioned methods such as wire mesh, pinholders, glass domes, etc. It comes in all shapes and sizes, and in different colours, and although I have my favourite, try them all to see which you prefer.*

Cut or carve the floral foam to the shape you require. It must be well soaked before it is wedged into position in the container and the arrangement is started. It takes roughly 20 minutes to soak (depending on size, of course), but as a guide, when the bubbles stop, it's ready to use. If the foam can be wedged into the container it will be firm; if not, tape it down with the special floral foam tape available from florists' sundries shops.

Always keep water in the container, and never let the foam dry out. Floral foam can be used more than once – you can turn a largish block over, to use the un-holed side – but it will have to be thrown out eventually.

Dri-foam Dri-foam is a catch-all name for a floral foam that is used dry, mainly for dried flower arrangements. I use it a lot, as you will see throughout my seasonal arrangements and ideas in general. The only thing to remember is not to soak it! Special pinholders are available to hold dri-foam in place, as it's so light without the water weight, and floral foam tape is useful too.

Containers

The containers – not vases, please – for flower arrangements can be anything and everything; basically, if it holds water, it holds flowers! I am sure if you look around your shelves and your cupboards you will come across many forgotten or ignored objects that could become containers for flowers. Indeed, if you become a collector, like me, you will soon be so surrounded that you'll need to move house to make room for everything!

I'm an inveterate collector of anything that takes my fancy and, as you will discover throughout the book, I use many things that are unusual, things that before the advent of modern mechanics like floral foam could only have been used with difficulty. The photographs will give you many ideas, and I outline a few basics below.

Obviously the traditional vase-shaped containers of glass, china, metal, etc can be used, but try to think of more unusual things. Individual glasses could look wonderful – a champagne glass with three roses, for instance; a beer mug, if less elegant, could look as good. Have a look around antique or junk shops for old china; even chipped items can be good for flowers as the chips can be hidden or disguised: old flan or pie dishes, soup bowls, sauce boats, jugs or soap dishes could all be the base for some sort of flower arrangement.

Metal containers can look splendid – the classic silver rose bowl, for instance, pewter jugs and bowls, old copper or brass saucepans, vegetable dishes, fish kettles, troughs or jelly moulds. Even well-polished metal plates – pewter is a favourite of mine, and I have a huge collection of pewter and Britannia metal tea and coffee pots – could look wonderful with a small arrangement in the middle. Don't forget about tall containers, either, such as candlesticks.

Other container fabrics are wood and basketry – my special favourite – and these, obviously, have to be treated slightly differently. They don't hold water, so need an inner lining which does. Collect plastic canisters (from washing-up liquid bottles), cups and cans of various sizes to accommodate different sizes of pinholders and floral foam. Apply several coats of matt green or black paint to these articles (you can use spray paint), allowing each coat to dry before applying the next. The paint prevents rusting of the metal cans, and the dark colours readily disappear in the shadows of the plant material. For flatter baskets or wooden boxes, you can use small baking trays or bread tins or flat glass dishes of the right size. You could also use soaked floral foam wrapped in polythene or plastic film. So, now you know about those basics, think about baskets with lids, with handles, wooden tea caddies, cigar boxes, picnic hampers, etc.

Have a look too at the photographs throughout the book – particularly the one on the back jacket, showing me with part (!) of my basketry collection – where you will recognize another kind of container, the more unusual varieties I mentioned earlier. With floral foam and judicious wiring, even occasional glueing or nailing, all sorts of things can be put to use: branches of interesting shapes, slices of old wood polished up a bit, straw or basketry mats, an interesting piece of flat stone, such as slate. Many of these are simply bases, rather than containers, on which an arrangement can be built. You can make your own bases from fibreboard too (see page 76), and, of course, in many arrangements, nothing of the container is seen at all, so anything could be used, from a plastic or china soap dish, to a priceless wine coaster or cheap saucer.

Basically, every flower arranger should look at the 'containing' potential of everything – in junk shops, kitchen shops, at jumble sales and auctions, both at home and abroad. The 'eye' develops with practice and you'll soon have a collection second to none (except mine, but then I've been at it for over twenty years!).

Conditioning of Plant Materials

You want flowers and foliage to look their best for use in arrangements, and you want them to stay looking their best. A little care from you will help. Proper conditioning before arranging will give more life to your arrangement, although some flowers just do last better than others, and no one can do much about that. You will soon pick up the ropes, get to know your materials through handling them, know what sort of treatment they want – and expect – and this only comes with practice. The principal rule and it must be adhered to, is to cut, pick or buy the day before arranging, and condition well before use.

Garden Plants *We all know that when flowers or foliage are cut they will die unless they get into water at the earliest opportunity. Always cut flowers and foliage from the garden in the morning or early evening, and take a bucket with you holding about 4-5in (10-12.5cm) of clean tap water. Don't think you have to take a full bucket with you (water is very heavy); a few inches will do for a start. Always cut flowers and foliage of all kinds with a slanting cut so that a larger area of drinking surface is exposed (it also prevents a stem slipping to the bottom of a container and creating a vacuum so that water can't get into the stem), and immediately they are cut put them in the bucket.*

When you get back to the house, fill the bucket with more water and leave the plant material for at least 12 hours, or overnight, in a cool place to have a good long drink. It is also important to remove all leaves that are below the water line; it's probable that you will be removing them anyway when you come to arrange the flowers or foliage, so you can remove them now.

Different types of plant need different treatment. If woody stems are cut (again, at an angle), either slit them up the stem for about 1in (2.5cm), crush them, or strip the bark off for about 1in (2.5cm) so that the white under-stem shows clearly, all before soaking. Some flowers with soft stems which exude a slimy sap – like hyacinths and narcissi – should be placed in water on their own until all the sap has seeped out, and then put into clean water to soak. Some stems of cut flowers bleed a milky substance (euphorbias and poppies, for instance): hold the cut tip of the stem over a flame – gas or candle – for a few seconds until the stem is sealed, then plunge stems into deep water overnight as usual.

Some flowers and foliages have to be treated with boiling water to start off with, and this is also the method by which you revive wilting flowers. Put about 3in (7.5cm) of boiling water into a bucket or old pan. Re-cut the stems and stand them in the water for about 1 minute, keeping the flower heads out of the steam. This method will remove an air lock and start the plant drinking again. After the minute is up, stand the flowers in deep cold water overnight; they will then be revivified, ready to arrange.

Gerbera (see page 15) is a flower that needs boiling water conditioning. Stand the newly-cut stems in about 3in (7.5cm) of boiling water in a bucket for about 20 seconds and then put them immediately into a tall straight-sided bucket of cold water to encourage the stems to go straight. Another way of straightening the stems after the 20-second treatment is to put the cold water into a small plastic dustbin with some wire mesh stretched across the top. Carefully poke the flower stems through the mesh until the heads rest flat on the mesh, and the stems dangle in the water. Leave them in the cold water to condition for 3 days – they will then last 3 weeks.

Florist Plants *People living in towns may have to rely on florists' flowers and foliage, and often you just can't be sure when the shop took delivery of them. Flowers and foliage also come into our markets from all the corners of the globe, so some of them can be suffering from a bit of 'jet lag'. Flowers offered to you by the florist should always be in peak condition, but you just never can tell. . . . If you are going out to buy flowers and are returning home immediately, that is fine, but, whatever you do, don't buy flowers and put them in the car or trail them round with you (they do not like being out of water). If you are well in with your florist, ask for the flowers to be kept in water until you collect them later – then get them home as soon as possible. Follow the conditioning instructions detailed above.*

Care of Arrangements *Care of your cut flowers and foliage should not stop once they're arranged. You want all your creative work to be admired for as long as possible, and there are still a few rules to follow. Arrangements of cut flowers and foliage – like people – don't like too much heat, or draughts: place them carefully, not too near heat sources, and away from leaky windows and outside doors. Cut flowers can drink a surprising amount of water, too, when arranged, even if conditioned properly first; so top up if you think it necessary, and never let floral foam dry out. A little fine mist sprayed over the arrangement occasionally will do the flowers no harm, just as it does most of your houseplants good. And don't ever dismiss old wives' tales about how to make flowers last – that aspirin could be just the job!*

Dried and Preserved Flowers *See page 101.*

The Principles of Flower Arranging
Flower arranging is a personal art and there really are no rules. As with everything, what is one man's meat is another's poison. Basically the flower arranger is creating a picture with flowers as an artist is with paint, and the end results can be as different as an abstract Picasso and a gentle Impressionist painting. You do what you like.

There are basic guidelines, though. The flowers used should be well conditioned, should be in different stages of development – buds, half-open, and full blooms – for interest, and should never be cut to the same length. Always have an in-and-out appearance, with recessed flowers to give a three-dimensional, not flat, appearance to the arrangement. Group flowers in different shapes and colours in sweeps, not blocks. Always examine your arrangement, and work on it from all the angles from which it will be seen; an arrangement for against a wall is quite different from one to be the centrepiece of a dinner table, which will be viewed from all sides. And, perhaps most important of all, let the plant materials themselves dictate to you what should be done with them. They were beautiful in their natural state; try to recreate that naturalness.

Colour *It is the colours of flowers that first catch the eye, and the colours of the setting and containers are also important, so it is worth giving colour some thought before starting an arrangement or setting. The colours of flowers give life to our surroundings, but if the wrong pink in a flower clashes with candles or cloth, instead of a glorious togetherness, you may end up with something you can barely live with. If you think the brown leaves of autumn look better with the peach-coloured flowers you have, think about whether a touch of lime green would give just a little light. Will those deep reds go dead in candlelight?*

In many cases it's a matter of experiment and experience. You will gradually become more aware of colour in everything; it's worth looking at a colour wheel and you will see what I mean. The main colours are red, orange, yellow, green, blue and violet – but it's all those other colours in between, the shades, tones and tints of those colours that you will start to see in your flowers and foliages. There are also neutral colours – black, white and grey – and these can be useful backgrounds for flowers, not affecting the colours in any way. Collect shade cards of artists' colours, house-paint colour charts, knitting wools and cottons, odd pieces of fabric and wallpaper. Then try the colours in various combinations: you will discover interesting, dramatic, subtle and pretty effects. Play about with them to see which give vibrant effects, which look dull, which change in daylight, artificial light and candlelight. Mother Nature combines her colours in some very remarkable ways, so study the flowers, leaves, branches, stones, shells, etc, and become more aware.

Colours can be used to give dramatic or gentle effects. Colours have personalities, just as people do: pale colours such as cream and yellow can be bright, pretty and youthful; reds can be exciting, rich and joyful; blues and greens can be clean, cool and very restful (blues can also disappear in the wrong lighting); white can be crisp and delicate. An arrangement of darker colours normally looks better on a pale background, and pale colours look effective against a dark background – but then again, rules are meant to be broken, and often too much of a contrast can spoil the finished effect.

The arrangements throughout the book have all been specifically designed to go with backgrounds – walls, screens, wallpapers, tablecloths, with the occasion itself – which are an integral part of the complete setting, the whole finished effect.

Remember, all facets of the art of flower arranging are essentially personal, and you will already have your own strong viewpoints – which I hope my ideas will enrich – or you will quickly learn, I hope, under my enthusiastic tutelage. The step-by-step pictures between pages 56 and 57 show the gradual build-up of a welcome arrangement for autumn, which will illustrate more clearly than words can how I arrange flowers.

1. The urn-shaped container of dark green pottery is one of my favourite shapes – it always seems to work. Start with the outline of the arrangement, to set the height and width. Make the first placement, the spine piece, which should be as straight and upright as possible to make the arrangement look firm. Place this well towards the back in the wedged-in piece of soaked floral foam, and follow this with the side-flowing berry sprays. The fruit foliage used for the outline is a variety of mountain ash (Sorbus hupehensis obtusa 'Rosea'), and it's followed by sweeping sprays of ivy (Hedera canariensis). These outline placements should radiate from the centre and look completely natural (use the curve of the material itself to advantage), so let it flow.

2. The outline of the arrangement is now more full. Sprays of an autumnal dark-leafed prunus foliage give depth of colour flowing through the arrangement, with some shorter pieces well recessed into the centre as camouflage for the floral foam. One of my favourite flowing foliages, the Nephrolepis, or ladder, fern brings a lovely movement as well as texture into the group; it's the forms and shapes that give the arrangement interest.

3. The flowers echoing the pink berry colour with which we started are now introduced. The tall straight gladioli follow the straight spine line of the sorbus. Never cut your flower stems until you know what length you need. That first straight one needs length; now grade the others down towards the centre of the arrangement, getting the weight of form and colour needed. The next flowers are now introduced – pink carnations and pink spray carnations – to keep up the gentle flow towards the sides. With flowers such as carnations, hold the flower two-thirds down the stem and let the flower itself dictate which way it wants to fall, whether left or right.

4. The centre of any massed arrangement is the most important, and the 'best', largest or darkest flowers should be placed here. The focal point of my arrangement is one of my top five favourite flowers – the gerbera. This daisy-like flower has been so developed over the past few years that the colour ranges are quite astounding. (It needs careful conditioning, so see page 12.) Because of the pink colour scheme, I have chosen the very soft coral pink gerbera ('Apple Blossom'), which goes well too with the 'Sonya' roses I have used. Having made sure there are no gaps, the arrangement is now ready to greet your guests.

Mountain ash (Sorbus hupehensis obtusa 'Rosea')
Ivy (Hedera canariensis)
Prunus
Nephrolepis fern
Gladiolus
Carnation and spray carnation
Gerbera ('Apple Blossom')
Rose ('Sonya')

Spring

Fruit
Apples · Apricots · Green gooseberries ·
Rhubarb

Vegetables
Asparagus · Carrots (young) · Cauliflower ·
Courgettes · Dandelion · Easterledge · Leeks
· Radishes · Spinach · Spring cabbage,
greens and onions · Watercress

Herbs
Borage · Chives · Dill · Fennel · Lovage ·
Marjoram · Mint · Sage · Tarragon

Spring

Garden and Florist Flowers

Anemone · Clivia · Daffodil · Freesia · Hyacinth · Iris ·
Lilac · Muscari (grape hyacinth) · Narcissus ·
Polyanthus · Tulip

All Season Flowers

Carnation (bloom and spray) · Spray Chrysanthemum
· Gladiolus · Lily · Rose

Blossom

Forsythia · Hamamelis mollis (witch hazel) ·
Hazel catkin · Jasminum nudiflorum (winter-
flowering jasmine) · Mimosa · Viburnum fragrans ·
Viburnum grandiflorum

Spring Food

The word spring conjures up the concepts of returning warmth, of fresh hope, new beginnings, and a renewal of life. As the days start to grow longer and the temperature rises, the first snowdrops appear, and when the daffodils glow with colour, we know spring has truly arrived.

My earliest memories of spring are of the farm just outside Carlisle where I was evacuated in 1942-44, when I found tadpoles, and drank the first milk from the cow after she'd given birth. It was supposed to have tremendous medicinal properties, but I didn't like it, just as I didn't like the brimstone and treacle forced down the throats of a myriad screaming children at that time of year. (Cleaning the system of winter ills is much better left to the joys of the first rhubarb, wiped clean and dipped into caster sugar and eaten whole!)

In this spring section the menus are based on the whole on salmon and lamb, as, in my opinion, the spring months of March, April and May are when both are at their best. The recipes concerned don't necessarily call for huge expense, as many use off-cuts or small quantities. I hope that they give you lots of ideas – and pleasure.

Apart from the true religious aspect of this season, centred on Easter, it is a time when many people seem to get married, so we have based our entertaining ideas on several occasions relevant to such festivities: I give ideas of what to serve at a small wedding buffet; of what the newly married couple might serve their parents for a first dinner party in their new home; as well as an informal housewarming supper. The Easter holiday itself calls for a relaxed and delicious breakfast, and it's a time to celebrate, having friends round for lunch.

Spring Flowers

Spring is probably – and perhaps surprisingly – the worst time of the year for the flower arranger. Flowers can always be bought from florists' shops, but foliage – an essential for good arrangements – can be difficult to obtain.

I think the ivy (hedera) family is about the best bet for any flower arranger, wherever he or she lives, and I grow quite a few varieties in my own garden. My favourite ivy is canariensis variegata, *with dark green in the centre, merging through silvergrey to a white border. Even the common ivy (hedera helix) is well worth a spot in the garden.*

It really surprises me how little interest is shown in that good old stand-by, the laurel, when considering foliage. I have five laurels in my garden, and find them useful in any season. One I would never be without is the spotted laurel (Aucuba japonica variegata). Laurus, the bay laurel or sweet bay much used by cooks, is also worth a place, and is a wonderful cut foliage.

One of the shrubs most popular with gardeners as well as flower arrangers is Elaeagnus. *It belongs to a large family, but of special interest is* Elaeagnus pungens maculata, *with its green and yellow blotches. Whatever the weather, it will always provide you with some foliage to cut and, on the dull days of winter, will give a glow of colour in the garden. It's slow growing, though.*

Mexican Orange Blossom or Choisya ternata *is a shrub that I think is not grown enough. The lovely dark glossy leaves are always a joy, and in early summer there is a scented white blossom. Again, not everyone likes the aromatic smell of the cut stem.*

Another shrub I would not be without in my garden is the Skimmia. It's rather slow growing for a flower arranger, so a little patience is need, as the shrub will never achieve any great size. In fact, I have only just started to cut mine, and it's been in my garden for years. Skimmia japonica Foremanii *is the one to go for; not only does it produce foliage, but it has creamy white flowers and red berries throughout the winter. Any shrub that is so useful in so many ways is well worth its place in the garden.*

The shrub that I think has surprised me most in my northern garden is Griselinia littoralis. *I think it's a fantastic foliage shrub – always lustrous yellow-green and so useful – and it can be picked all year round.*

I wonder how many of you grow the golden privet (Ligustrum ovalifolium aureo-marginatum). I think this is a much underrated shrub which should be grown more often as a specimen type shrub than as the usual hedge. If left to grow on instead of being given its fortnightly clipping, it makes very useful arching foliage. The fortunate thing about this shrub compared with the skimmia is that it grows much more quickly.

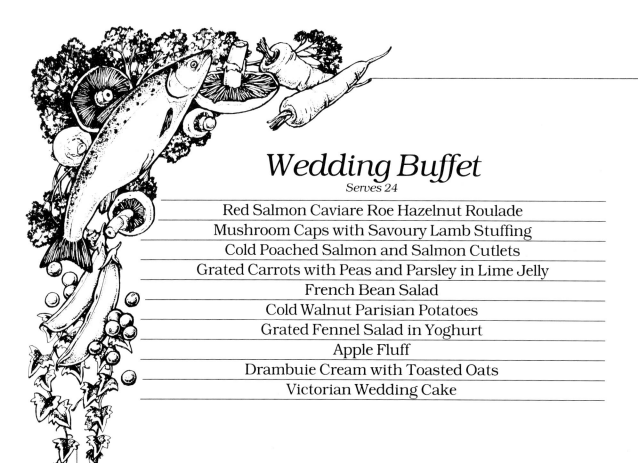

Wedding Buffet
Serves 24

Red Salmon Caviare Roe Hazelnut Roulade

Mushroom Caps with Savoury Lamb Stuffing

Cold Poached Salmon and Salmon Cutlets

Grated Carrots with Peas and Parsley in Lime Jelly

French Bean Salad

Cold Walnut Parisian Potatoes

Grated Fennel Salad in Yoghurt

Apple Fluff

Drambuie Cream with Toasted Oats

Victorian Wedding Cake

Early on in my catering career the run-up to the end of the tax year in April was, I think, the main reason why wedding receptions were so popular. Nowadays I don't think there are any tax advantages in getting married at this time of year, but it is still a time when many people choose to marry. And as it can prove to be such an expensive occasion, I have given you splendid buffet recipes which can almost all be prepared in advance. The whole salmon – beautifully decorated with scored cucumber slices and then topped off with thin aspic – is time-consuming to prepare, so you may prefer to cook the salmon in the alternative fashion, as cutlets. The red salmon caviare roulade looks wonderful, and will probably be the talking point of the display. The stuffed mushroom caps are tasty and filling, and the two salads are unusual but delicious. You can, if you like, add more run-of-the-mill accompaniments, such as hard-boiled eggs, radishes and dressed peas, for instance, but I have deliberately tried to avoid the norm and given you more adventurous ideas and recipes that, as well as going well together, can be prepared in advance.

Many of you will prefer to have your cake baked for you, but if you are prepared to tackle this marathon on your own, I give you a simple recipe for a delicious cake.

Red Salmon Caviare Roe Hazelnut Roulade

Caviare is a weakness of mine, and often when I go mad and order some I think I am weak in the head when I realize how expensive it is. But I have discovered American red salmon caviare roe and it is oily, tasty and good – and cheaper. It can be bought in Harrods and Fortnums, and keeps for some time in the refrigerator.

If you want to know more in detail about making roulades, see Entertaining with Tovey. *Basically, remember that the lighter, the more successful, so beat up the yolks and the whites as much as possible. The principal problem is the turning out, so you must line your 12 x 8in (30 x 20cm) roulade trays – two of them – with the best quality silicone greaseproof paper. Staple the paper corners together, and brush with olive oil.*

First make the 2 roulades. Pre-heat the oven to 350°F (180°C), Gas 4.

Separate 4 of the eggs, and beat the yolks in a warmed bowl for several minutes. Very slowly add the ginger, salt and sugar, and beat well together.

Separate the remaining eggs, put the yolks to one side, and beat the 6 egg whites until stiff in a clean bowl. Gently fold one-third of the stiff egg whites into the yolk mixture. Beat up the remaining egg whites again, and fold into the yolky mixture. Finally, fold in the hazelnuts very gently.

Turn into the prepared trays and bake in the pre-heated oven for about 12-15 minutes. Check that they are done by inserting a skewer quickly; if it comes out dry, the roulades are ready.

When cold, turn out carefully onto a foil and greaseproof paper covered board a little larger than the tray. Beat the cream cheese with the 2 remaining egg yolks and double cream, and then gently fold in the salmon caviare roe. Spread this mixture liberally over the roulades, and then roll up carefully.

Two roulades would normally serve 12 people for a starter. Cut these more thinly and they will allow a portion for each of 24 guests – but some may, of course, be quite happy with the mushrooms as starter...

Makes 2 roulades
6 eggs
¼ tsp ginger
½ tsp onion salt
1oz (25g) soft brown sugar
6oz (175g) ground hazelnuts, sieved
1lb (450g) cream cheese
4 tbsp double cream
4oz (100-125g) American red salmon caviare roe

Mushroom Caps with Savoury Lamb Stuffing

1 lb (450 g) lean shoulder of lamb
3 oz (75 g) onion, finely chopped
1 tbsp cooking oil
3 oz (75 g) butter
1 clove juicy garlic, crushed with
    ½ tsp salt
½ tbsp tomato purée
½ tbsp each of chopped parsley
    and marjoram
¼ tbsp ground coriander
1 egg
24 large mushroom caps, without
    stalks

Chop the lamb into cubes, cutting off excess fat, and then put twice through the mincer. Fry the onion in the oil and ½ oz (15 g) of the butter for a minute or two, then add the garlic and salt, lamb, tomato purée, parsley, marjoram and coriander. Cook for 10 minutes, remove from the heat and cool slightly.

Put the cooked lamb mixture into your food processor or blender with the egg, and blend together for a few minutes. This makes a pleasant smooth texture, but a rougher textured mixture can still be used.

Fry the mushroom caps (skinned if necessary) in the remaining butter and leave to drain. When both are cold, pipe the lamb mixture into the mushroom caps and arrange on a serving dish.

Cold Poached Salmon

Fish stock, per 1 pt (600 ml) water
2 tbsp olive oil
1 tsp wine vinegar
4 peppercorns
6 stalks fresh parsley
1 tsp salt
a few onion rings
1 chopped carrot

Cold poached salmon is the most delicious spring dish of all – indeed I would eat it all year round if I could. To poach a salmon in an 'S' position, which creates the illusion of the fish swimming, it is essential that you have a large fish kettle. An expensive item, I must admit, but less of a short-season luxury now with farmed salmon becoming more and more popular and easily available most of the year. You also need four half bricks, which you wrap in double thicknesses of foil.

Weigh the fish – a portion of 6 oz (175 g) per person is generous for a filling fish like salmon – then gut it well and wash in running cold water. Carefully place it bellyside down on to the drop-tray in the fish kettle. Fill the kettle with measured water until the salmon is covered, then take out the salmon and the drop-tray. Add the fish stock ingredients to the water in the kettle, per each pint (600 ml) of measured water, and bring to the boil. Meanwhile arrange the salmon on the tray. Place the first half brick by the head to guide it in the first turn of the 'S', and the second on the other side; the third brick should go half way along the belly and the last on the opposite side of the tail. This holds it in the rough 'S' shape.

When the stock has simmered for 5 minutes, immerse the tray and the salmon in it. Allow to cook for 1 minute per pound (450 g) only. Leave to go absolutely cold in the water and then take the drop-tray out of the stock. Skin the fish using a small palette or stainless-steel knife; it should come off very easily but care is needed, particularly when removing the dark brown substance attached to the skin.

You can, if you like, glaze the fish as it is with white wine aspic, but with about half an hour's intensive work you can re-create a glimmering skin appearance by using very, very thin slices of scored cucumber plus the aspic. Place the first layer of cucumber slices below the neck coming from the belly up over the back and on to the opposite side. Dip each slice into the cooling aspic and it should stick fairly easily to the flesh, but if you are experiencing difficulty, toothpicks chopped in half will hold the slices in position until the aspic sets. Carry on down the back towards the tail, overlapping each slice with half of the next to make it look more like scales (see the photograph between pages 56 and 57). Coat finally with aspic – you'll need about 1 pt (600 ml) – in the same way as the cutlets.

Poached Salmon Cutlets

Each salmon cutlet should weigh at least 4 oz (100-125 g) and preferably going on 6 oz (175 g) for a generous portion. I prefer to have them prepared in cutlets minus the bone so you buy the salmon by the fillet (which resembles sides of smoked salmon) but don't let the fishmonger discard the head, tail and skin, etc. as you need these for the stock.

For 12 cutlets
head, tail and bones of the fish
2 pt (1.2 l) cold water
1 pt (600 ml) white wine
8 tbsp olive oil
16 black peppercorns
6 large sprigs fresh parsley
juice of 2 fresh lemons
1 tsp sea salt

Put all the stock ingredients into a saucepan, bring to the boil, and simmer gently for about 8 minutes.

Place the 12 cutlets of salmon in well-buttered roasting trays and pass the simmering stock through a strainer all over them. Put a generous dab of butter on each cutlet, and cover the whole tray with doubled foil. Bring back to simmering point on top of the stove, and cook for 4 minutes only. Remove from heat and leave to get cold. Remove cutlets from the liquid, and arrange on cooling trays placed over trays of about 1 in (2.5cm) in depth.

Garnish each cutlet with thin shreds of various vegetables and other goodies, and arrange them into flower and other shapes. Use thin slices of scored cucumber, red pepper skins, thin slices of skinned tomato and hard-boiled eggs, along with lovely sprays of fresh fennel or dill or parsley (the photograph between pages 56 and 57 should give you an idea of what I mean).

Aspic

I always use commercial aspic, but I never follow the instructions properly. For salmon – whole or cutlets – I would make up 1 pt (600 ml) with half water and half inexpensive white wine. Simmer the aspic according to the packet instructions, cool, and as it begins to set, spoon with a large tablespoon over each cutlet (what doesn't adhere will fall through onto the tray below and can be used again).

It will take patience, care and time to build up a lovely, obvious thickness of glaze. You will have to put the finely coated cutlets on the cooling tray into the fridge to set; you will have to keep the aspic just nice and runny; and as the first and subsequent layers set on the cutlets, you will have to repeat it all. However long it takes, it will look most effective, and you will feel very clever as your guests congratulate you on your effort.

Grated Carrots with Peas and Parsley in Lime Jelly

Serves 24
2-3 packets lime jelly
olive oil
1 lb (450 g) carrots, finely grated
1 lb (450 g) frozen peas
2 bunches parsley, finely chopped

Use packets of good commercial lime jelly, but only use two-thirds of the liquid stipulated on the packet. Melt the jelly first and leave to one side in a large jug with a good pouring lip.

I make these in ice-cube trays with 12 or 16 partitions. Estimate roughly how much jelly you need for your trays by filling them with water, then measuring the amount of water. You won't need quite as much as you've measured, as the vegetables will take up some of the volume.

Paint the trays with good olive oil before putting a thin coating of the jelly into the base of each. Put this in the fridge to set while you prepare the vegetables. Finely grate some sweet carrots, just barely cook some frozen peas, and coarsely chop some parsley. The dish can be varied by including or substituting finely diced red pepper, cucumber, apple, fennel, etc.

As the balance of the jelly in the jug is about to set, fold in the grated carrots with the peas and parsley. This is poured into the ice-cube trays on top of the set thin layer, and put back in the fridge.

These jellies look very pretty on many salad or cold dishes, and are delicious and refreshing.

French Bean Salad

This is not a seasonal dish as such, as Kenyan French beans are readily available throughout the year. They go so well with the salmon too.

Bring 6 pts (3.4 l) lightly salted water to the boil, and throw in the lovingly topped and tailed beans (occasionally they have a light string down their sides, and this should also be removed). Simply bring back to the boil, then drain off the water and refresh the beans under very cold water. Leave to drain.

Arrange the beans decoratively on the plates — if you've time, in a trellis shape. Leave to one side, and just before serving, season generously with the pepper. Whizz all the dressing ingredients around in your blender, and pour over the beans at the very last minute.

For 24
2 lb (900 g) French beans
pinch of salt
freshly ground black pepper

Dressing
6 tbsp olive oil
2 tbsp white wine
1 tsp white wine vinegar
½ tsp caster sugar

Cold Walnut Parisian Potatoes

At first sight this recipe may appear very extravagant as you need so many individual potatoes to give you so few Parisian balls! But, of course, the holey shape left behind isn't wasted, as you can cook it later and make into creamed potatoes.

If you use the recommended weight of potatoes, you will get about 6 Parisian balls per guest. Wash and peel the potatoes and then make the balls with a Parisian scoop. Put the balls into a saucepan of cold water, add the salt, and bring to the boil. Drain through a strainer and refresh under a cold running tap.

Coat a couple of baking trays (approximately 14 × 8in or 35 × 20cm) thickly with the soft butter. Place the potatoes into the trays and then bake in the oven at 450°F (230°C), Gas 8 for 30 minutes. Lift out with a slotted spoon and drain thoroughly on kitchen paper. Leave to cool.

When you wish to serve them, paint them with walnut oil and arrange in a couple of dishes. Sprinkle with chopped parsley and grated cheese if you like.

For 24
10 lb (4.6 kg) potatoes
2 tbsp salt
1 lb (450 g) soft butter
walnut oil
chopped parsley and Parmesan cheese to garnish

Grated Fennel Salad in Yoghurt

Serves 24

at least 4 lb (1.8 kg) fennel bulbs
1 tsp fennel seeds
2 tsp salt
1 pt (600 ml) natural yoghurt

You need so much fennel because the outer leaves tend to be rather stringy and dirty. Remove these, but for goodness sake don't throw them away, as they are ideal for making stock or soup. Carefully remove the lovely green feathery tops of the fennel and retain. Grate the bulbs on the coarse side of a grater (do not use an electric grater).

In a pestle and mortar grind together the fennel seeds and salt. Put the grated fennel into bowls and combine with the yoghurt, fennel seeds and salt. Turn out the bowl shapes onto plates, and garnish with the feathery fennel tops.

This makes approximately 24 tablespoons of salad, which is enough per person in combination with the vegetables and other salad.

Apple Fluff

For 12

12 Granny Smith apples
8 oz (225 g) caster sugar
4 egg whites
4 oz (100-125 g) sultanas, soaked overnight in 4 tbsp dark rum
grated rind of 1 orange, or toasted pine kernels

This makes an economical ending to a splendid buffet. Allow 1 apple per person.

Wipe the apples and place them in a baking tray with just enough water to cover the bottom. Bake at 400°F (200°C), Gas 6 for 45 minutes (turning the apples over after 25 minutes) or until the apples are nice and tender. Do not cook them to the stage when they are literally falling apart.

Remove the apples from the tray and scoop out the delicious flesh. Discard the skin and core. Liquidize the apples with half the caster sugar, and leave to cool. Beat the egg whites to a dry white mass and then little by little add the remaining sugar (this can all be done in a mixer). Fold the rum-sodden sultanas into the soft apple and mix evenly.

Combine the stiff egg whites with the apple mixture and sultanas, and spoon into 12 glasses. Sprinkle each glass with the grated orange rind or, even better, toasted pine kernels.

Drambuie Cream with Toasted Oats

This is very similar to the crème part of a crème brûlée, but is much more delicious, and makes a superb climax to a lovely occasion. This recipe will fill 10 × 3in (7.5cm) ramekins but, as it is so rich, I think I would be tempted to pour the pud into sherry glasses, which will give you practically double portions.

Please don't be put off by the amount of cream, as it truly is memorable, and will send all your guests home happy.

Whisk the eggs, sugar and Drambuie together in a small bowl that will sit on top of one of your saucepans. Put the bowl in the pan over simmering water and cook for 15 minutes, stirring from time to time, until the mixture thickens.

Put the cream in a large saucepan and pass the egg mixture through a plastic sieve into the cream. Beat vigorously with an electric hand mixer or rotary whisk. Put the pan partially over a very gentle heat, and simmer for about 25 minutes. Whatever you do, do ensure that only half of the pan is in contact with the heat (or use an asbestos mat), otherwise the cream will boil over. After 25 minutes, the mixture will have thickened and reduced by approximately one-third.

Remove from heat, cool a little, and pass again through a plastic sieve. Pour into individual dishes.

Meanwhile, spread the porridge oats over a baking tray and bake in the oven at 350°F (180°C), Gas 4 for 15 minutes, turning over from time to time. When nicely browned, sprinkle immediately on top of the individual dishes and put aside to chill.

Serves 10-15
2 eggs
4 oz (100-125 g) caster sugar
¼ pt (150 ml) Drambuie (plus, as an option, Drambuie in the base of each container)
2 pts (1.1 l) double cream
3 oz (75 g) porridge oats

Victorian Wedding Cake

Fills an 11-12in (27.5-30cm) round tin

1 lb (450 g) sultanas
3 lb (1.4 kg) currants
¼ pt (150 ml) cooking brandy
¼ pt (150 ml) dark rum
juice and rind of 1 lemon
1 lb (450 g) butter
14 oz (400 g) dark brown soft sugar
1 lb, 4 oz (550 g) eggs (see method)
12 oz (350 g) each of citron and orange peel, finely chopped
2 oz (50 g) nibbed almonds
1 lb (450 g) plain flour, sieved
pinch of salt
½ tsp each of grated nutmeg, mixed spice and powdered mace

I am hopeless, helpless, gormless and daft when it comes to trying to ice cakes in a professional manner. Time after time I have tried to master this art, to no avail. So I'll leave the decoration to your other favourite books. I do love rich fruit cakes, though.

The following recipe is a basic one handed down from a relative to my grandmother, and although I give it as a wedding cake it is equally good topped off with whole almonds and glacé cherries and served at a festive high tea. This cake should be made at least 3-4 weeks prior to being decorated, and only the finest ingredients should be used.

The day before cooking the cake, soak the sultanas and currants in the brandy and rum with the lemon juice and rind. It is important that the fruit be fresh and succulent; never, whatever you do, use old dried sultanas and currants.

Your loose-bottomed cake tin needs special preparation. Line it first with good heavy brown paper and then a layer of the finest greaseproof paper available. Put the greaseproof paper on top of the brown paper and then place the loose bottom of the cake tin on top and draw round it. Cut the pencilled circle out, but adding on about 1¼in (3cm) all round. At ½in (1.25cm) intervals snick this overlap just to the pencilled circle. This means that when you place the brown and greaseproof paper circles on the base inside the tin, the snicked edges will bend up the sides, thus forming a secure and leakproof base. Grease the sides of the tin and cut a thickness of brown paper and greaseproof paper to go round this and slightly overlap; where it overlaps, stick together with more grease.

To make the cake, have the butter at room temperature, break it up, and put in a large bowl. Add the sugar and beat away (I use a hand whisk) until the mixture is light and fluffy: this will take at least 10 minutes, and do beat away for that time, as this base is most important.

You might think I'm mad by saying that you require 1 lb, 4 oz (550 g) of eggs but this is the best amount for this recipe, and is the weight of the eggs out of their shells. You will need between 9 and 11 eggs. Lightly beat the eggs and then start to beat into the sugar/butter mixture a little at a time — if you add too much too quickly the mixture could curdle towards the end (not a disaster, though). Fold in the soaked sultanas and currants (which should, by now, have absorbed most of the booze) along with the citron and orange peel and almonds. Now gently fold in the sieved flour and salt, which have been mixed with the spices.

Transfer mixture to the cake tin and, using a spatula or large tablespoon, carefully draw the mixture from the middle up to the sides, to make a concave shape. If you know your oven tends to be fierce, cover the top of the tin with a single thickness of tinfoil (making sure it overlaps way over the outside) and cut a large circle in the middle of this the size of a coffee saucer. This will stop the top scorching. And, to be on the safe side, put a triple thickness of brown paper on the baking tray and place the tin on top of this.

The oven should be pre-heated to 275°F (140°C), Gas 1, and the cake should be baked for 6 hours. Gently open door of the oven and test with a meat skewer to see if done. Remove from oven and allow to cool for a while, then turn out onto a cooling tray. If feeling generous, when the cake is absolutely cold, paint with some more rum and brandy, and then wrap up completely in greaseproof paper and store in an old sweet tin in which you have pierced a few small holes to allow a little air in.

Wedding Buffet

Spring is when a young man's fancy 'turns to love', so they say, and what better than to start with a spring wedding. Impending wedding bells send shivers of excitement through every mother and dread through every father – but what a flower occasion!

The type of flower decoration for your wedding will, of course, depend upon the type of reception. We have chosen an informal buffet rather than a sit-down meal, and the flower arrangements have been carefully planned to fit in with this. The most important thing to remember is that the flowers must be lifted away from the food. A long low arrangement, although ideal for the length of a table at which people are sitting down, is not the best flower arrangement for a buffet: there's less room for the food, and it could get knocked over when people lean across.

Lifts – a means of lifting the flowers off the table – can be created by covering a firm box with the same colour fabric as the cloth (the same principle as bases, see page 76), but I prefer my flower arrangements in a visible container, such as the glass and gilt stands in the wedding buffet photograph. These were never in fact designed for flowers – they are floor-standing ashtrays about 20in (50cm) high! The ash bowl on the top is ideal for holding the soaked floral foam, and I used candles, as I thought candlelight would add considerably to the atmosphere.

I've used two arrangements simply because I had two matching containers! Glass, gilt and silver are all suitable for this more formal setting, and you can get the required height by using a tiered cake stand, tall containers or candlesticks.

To make the arrangement, anchor the floral foam in place with floral foam tape, and then place your candles. The easiest way of achieving this is to use special floral foam candle holders, or you can tape three wooden cocktail sticks to the end of the candle with half of the stick protruding beyond the candle to create a tripod effect. If you are doing two matching arrangements, do them in tandem, one piece or effect at a time, so that they match.

Place your outline foliage in next to give the outline dimension of the finished arrangement. I used sprays of ivy (hedera) and Berberis Virescens for this, and ivy (hedera canariensis) for the larger foliage in the centre. The flowers are spray carnations, Carol roses, Alstromeria (Peruvian lily), carnations, and single Bonnie Jean spray chrysanthemums. For lightness, sprays of Bristol Fairy complete the picture. Do make sure that the plant materials aren't arranged too near the candles!

For a party like this, a swagged table looks superb, and it's very easy to do (see pages 145 and 158).

Candles
Ivy
Berberis Virescens
Carnations and spray carnations
Roses ('Carol')
Alstromeria
Spray chrysanthemums
Bristol Fairy

Wedding Cake Garlands

The cake is a very traditional and important part of the reception, and can be a great decorative feature. Instead of, or as well as, iced decoration, you could add a cake-top arrangement, and some flowing garlands, both of which can be made with artificial flowers, and are very easy to do. The arrangement could be of lilies of the valley, white roses and stephanotis, arranged in some dri-foam in a small plastic container, and the top ends of the finished garland spine wires hook into the edge of this central top arrangement.

1. The making of a garland is easy if you remember that the main thing is to keep all your various materials in neat order. You will need approximately 15 flowers and 10 leaves per foot (30cm) of garland.

2. Each item you use needs a wire attached to it, to create a false stem. Holding a leaf, for instance, in one hand, back side facing upwards, take a silver wire and pierce either side of the main vein about half way up the leaf from the base. The stitch showing on the main side of the leaf should be small, so as not to spoil the leaf's visual look. Bring both ends of the wire down to the base of the leaf, keeping the looped top of the wire under your thumb nail. With the other hand take one of these wire legs and wind it around the other clockwise, catching the natural leaf stem. About 3 turns should do. The looped top of the wire now supports the back of the leaf and can give it shape if necessary. Prepare all your leaves in this way, and do the same with the flowers. Make a hairpin shape, the loop again held under the thumb nail against the side of the flower, and wind one wire leg around the other.

3. The next step is to tape the stems of the flowers and leaves. Lay the tape over the wire just behind the leaf or flower head and, using the thumb and forefinger, twist the stem to catch the loose end of the tape. Turn the stem and spiral the tape. Take the tape down about two-thirds of the stem length and break off (the tape is not sticky, it's the warmth of the hands and the stretching that do the sticking).

4. The next stage is to build up the garland. Having wired and taped all the individual items and arranged them into neat groups, take a thicker stub wire, which will be the spine wire, and select your first item. Lay the item against the spine at an angle and overtape the tape, twisting the wire and spiralling the tape (about two turns). This movement traps the item against the main spine wire.

5. Lay on your second item and repeat down the spine wire. Pick up different items each time to make the garland varied and interesting. Tape it down. Make about three or four garlands to surround the cake, depending on its size, of course.

Housewarming Supper
Serves 12

Minced Lamb Herb Patties or Sherried Lamb Loaf

Salmon Cream Pies with Peas

Rich Chocolate Squares

Rhubarb Fool

What a wonderful occasion this should be – the first party after all the rigmarole of the wedding ceremony, the reception, and moving into the new house after the honeymoon.

The supper is simple, but go to town on the actual presentation of your three courses, and stage-manage the whole event between the two of you so that it all runs smoothly. In fact, I strongly recommend that you have a 'dress rehearsal' the weekend before, actually trying out the recipes and deciding what is to go on what china, what cutlery you will use, and what serving dishes will be needed. Don't think that you need be limited to using only one set of china; if you've been given more than one set, use different plates for each course. Show off a bit!

The food should be no problem, but there are a few other hints to add to the success of your party. Never forget the bathroom: double check that there is enough paper, that there are hand towels, and fresh soap in the basin. Bulbs also have a nasty habit of popping on the day of a party, so ensure you have spares. Make sure that before you actually start the meal there is ample space in the kitchen for the dirty plates, and when clearing them, pile them up neatly, as they take up much less room this way. Oh yes, and don't forget to actually lay the coffee tray and have it close to hand for a flourishing end to the meal.

I have given you a choice of starters and puddings: serve either the Lamb Patties or the Meat Loaf; you can of course serve both Chocolate Squares and Rhubarb Fool!

Minced Lamb Herb Patties

Melt butter and fry the onion for a few moments before adding the grated carrots, and all the other ingredients (except the pastry and egg). Mix together well and cook for about 20 minutes.

Roll out the pastry to about ¼in (6mm) thickness, and cut out 48 circles of 3in (7.5cm) in diameter. Gently press 24 of the rings into greased patty tins. Divide the lamb mixture evenly between the 24 pastry bases, and then paint around the edges with the beaten egg. Place the other pastry circles on top, and seal the edges together with a small 4-prong fork. Put in the refrigerator to chill, or you could freeze them at this stage if you wanted.

When you wish to cook, pre-heat oven to 475°F (240°C), Gas 9, put the trays in the oven and immediately turn down to 450°F (230°C), Gas 8. Bake for 15 minutes and then take out of the oven. Remove from the patty tins, turning them upside down onto a plain baking tray. Return to oven and bake for a further 5 minutes or so. Serve hot or cold.

Makes 24 small patties
2 oz (50 g) butter
1 medium onion, finely chopped
2 medium carrots, finely grated
1 lb (450 g) lean shoulder of lamb, minced
1 tsp curry powder
6 dried apricots, finely chopped
4 tbsp pine kernels, toasted (optional)
1 tbsp tomato purée
2 tbsp finely chopped parsley
salt and freshly ground black pepper
1 lb (450 g) puff pastry
1 egg, lightly beaten

Sherried Lamb Loaf

This is an extremely pleasant moist meat loaf which slices quite easily, especially when cold, although it can be served hot.

Soak the sultanas and porridge oats in the sherry overnight. The next day, lightly fry the onion in the mutton fat or butter, then add the garlic and cook until onion is golden. Meanwhile, thoroughly mix all other ingredients, except the mustard, together in a large bowl. Fold in the cooked onion and garlic, and the soaked sultanas and oats.

Paint the sides of a 2 lb (900 g) loaf tin with the Moutarde de Meaux, and fill tin with the lamb mixture. (If there is any left over, leave to one side, and fry for supper.)

Pre-heat oven to 375°F (190°C), Gas 5. Place the loaf tin in a roasting tray partly filled with boiling water and cook for 1 hour. Turn the oven off, but leave the loaf in until the oven cools. Remove and, when cold, store in the refrigerator

Serves 12
4 oz (100-125 g) sultanas
4 oz (100-125 g) porridge oats
¼ pt (150 ml) medium sherry
1 large onion, finely diced
4 oz (100-125 g) mutton fat or butter
4 cloves garlic, crushed with 2 tsp salt
1 lb, 12 oz (750 g) lean shoulder of lamb, minced
2 medium eggs, lightly beaten
1 tsp each of black pepper, ground coriander and grated nutmeg
1 tsp fresh chopped thyme
1 tbsp each of fresh chopped marjoram and chives
4 tbsp fresh chopped parsley
2 tbsp tomato purée
5 tbsp Moutarde de Meaux

Salmon Cream Pies with Peas

Serves 12
18 oz (500 g) salmon
4 oz (100-125 g) butter
¾ pt (425 ml) rich white sauce
2 tbsp finely chopped parsley
8 oz (225 g) creamed potatoes
6 oz (175 g) frozen peas, defrosted

Salmon is definitely the best fish to serve at this time of year, but it needn't be expensive. A kindly fishmonger can sell you cheaper tail pieces to use in this dish, as a large proportion of it is made up of sauce, the mashed potatoes piped round the sides, and the peas in the middle. It's an ideal recipe for a small buffet, as each person has an individual plate and the pies are easily eaten with a fork. Serve with a good green or mixed salad.

Poach the salmon (see page 22) and then flake. Make sure there are no bones left. Melt about half the butter and lightly grease the sides and bottom of 12 oval or round ramekins. Divide the flaked boneless salmon between them. Coat with the rich white sauce, and sprinkle with the parsley.

Fill your piping bag with the creamed potatoes, and with a star nozzle, pipe the potatoes round the edges of the dishes. Fill the centre with the defrosted peas, cooked in a little water for a few minutes with some sugar.

When you want to serve the pies, warm through in a pre-heated oven at 350°F (180°C), Gas 4 for 12 minutes. Serve topped with knobs of butter.

Rich Chocolate Squares

6 oz (175 g) good plain chocolate
¼ pt (150 ml) dark rum
6 oz (175 g) soft brown sugar
6 oz (175 g) ground almonds
2 tbsp fine white breadcrumbs
6 eggs, separated
pinch of salt

Icing
1 lb (450 g) icing sugar
2 tbsp drinking chocolate
hot water to mix

Line a roasting tin approximately 14 × 10in (35 × 25cm) with a double thickness of greased greaseproof paper, and pre-heat the oven to 350°F (180°C), Gas 4.

In the top of a double boiler melt the chocolate with the rum over a medium heat. When quite smooth add the sugar, ground almonds and breadcrumbs, and cook, stirring with a wooden spoon, for 2 minutes. Allow to cool.

Beat the egg whites stiff with the pinch of salt. When the chocolate mixture is cool, beat in the egg yolks one at a time, and then turn out into a plastic bowl. Gently fold in the stiff egg whites a little at a time. The mixture will be quite stiff and 'orrible, but do not despair.

Spoon it out into the lined tin, smooth, and bake for 45 minutes. Leave in the tin to cool, and then turn out onto a board and cut into whatever size of square you like. (If you pack in airtight containers they will remain remarkably moist for some time.)

Split and fill with whipped cream or peanut butter (very fattening this way, but oh, so good). To make the icing, mix together the icing sugar and chocolate, and stir in enough hot water to make a thickish consistency. Spread over each square allowing it to drip down the sides, and decorate as you please – with walnut halves, glacé cherries, chocolate butter icing, etc.

Rhubarb Fool

My Nan always used to say that 'a person who just mixes stewed fruit with whipped cream and calls it a fool is a fool.' A real country fool should be made up of equal parts of rich cream and home-made egg custard with the purée of any fruit available. This rhubarb fool is a favourite of mine, especially if a little finely chopped preserved ginger is added.

Serves 12
2 lb (900 g) rhubarb
¼ pt (150 ml) water
¾ lb (350 g) caster sugar
*½ pt (300 ml) double cream,
    whipped*

Custard
½ pt (300 ml) milk
1 tsp cornflour
2 tbsp caster sugar
4 egg yolks
a little vanilla extract

Wipe the sticks of rhubarb, chop off the root ends, and cut into even pieces. Place in a clean saucepan with the water and caster sugar, and simmer over a low heat until the rhubarb 'falls'. Liquidize and pass through a plastic sieve – the rhubarb is some-times unusually stringy, but do persevere.

Meanwhile in the top half of a double boiler, mix the milk for the custard with the cornflour and sugar and bring to the boil. Re-duce the heat immediately. Lightly beat the egg yolks together and then beat into the hot milk little by little, stirring constantly with a wooden spoon until thick. Remove from heat and pass through a fine plastic sieve into a cold bowl. (Traditionally cornflour should not be used in a custard of this type, but it acts beautifully as a stabilizer ensuring that the mixture doesn't curdle. But, to be safe, all the time you are stirring, keep your eyes on the mixture, and if there is the slightest fear that it is going to split, remove from the heat at once!)

When the custard is cold, combine it with the vanilla extract, purée of rhubarb and then beat in the double cream. At this stage, if you like preserved ginger, lightly dice some and fold into the mixture. Spoon it out into glasses and leave to chill.

Gooseberry Fool
When gooseberries come in to season, gooseberry fool is delicious, and is made in exactly the same way, using 3 lb (1.4 kg) gooseberries. For a delicious flavour, add 2 tablespoons dried elderflowers to the cooking gooseberries.

Housewarming Supper

Having had that wonderful day – the wedding – it is now a question of getting down to reality and sorting out your first home. You will probably even be considering your first party, although you may not be completely ready. Even if funds have all been spent on more essential items such as wallpaper and paint, why not just say what the heck, they must take us as they find us – unpapered wall and all.

Simplicity must be the key word here, with both food and flowers, and as for the floral decoration, all that is needed is a bunch of daffodils, together with some pieces of foliage and blossom (see photograph between pages 56 and 57). You may not have got any candlesticks as yet, but candles and flowers are pleasant companions, and I am sure that empty bottles won't be difficult to find!

Get them in various sizes and wash the labels off. I have used four green bottles and to save money again I bought 2 of the longest green candles I could find and cut them in half – half in each bottle – which was cheaper than buying 4 candles. Ensure that the candles are firm in the bottle necks – trim with a knife to fit and secure with a little melted wax. I also found an old piece of green candle, lit it, and let it drip down the new candles in the bottles. This gives a more natural look and it does save the proper candles to burn throughout the party (and they must burn; you can't expect your guests to look at those unlit candles all night). A little tip here: always warm the bottles first when dripping the wax because it sticks better to warm glass, sometimes peeling away from cold glass.

Place a flat plastic dish holding soaked floral foam in the centre of your base (I used a round green linen base – see page 76 for instructions on how to make these yourself – but a tray will do). With some floral foam tape, go across the plastic dish and the soaked foam as if doing up a parcel with string. This holds the foam in place. Group the bottles around the dish with the taller ones towards the back, leaving spaces between the bottles for the flowers and foliage to come through. Now lay the grapes onto the base, having first cut the bunches into more manageable sizes (you don't want the first fruit picker to get the lot), and intersperse them with some green apples. Lead them in towards the foam so that they look as if they are flowing out of the arrangement.

The first placement of plant material was winter jasmine (Jasminum) with its delicate bright yellow blossom, which starts to flower long before Christmas in many parts of the country. Start high up at the back with the first placement, grading the stems down towards the centre. Flow some pieces to the sides between the bottles, all the time remembering to keep the plant materials away from the candle tops. To strengthen the jasmine line I have used laurel (Laurus), following the shape I initiated with the

Bottles
Candles
Grapes
Apples
Winter jasmine
Laurel
Daffodils

jasmine. Use some individual leaves from the laurel to cover the floral foam and to soften the round shape of the apples. Now you have only your bunch of daffodils (usually 10 or 12), and each flower has to count. Start again at the top and grade the flower stems down towards the centre. Measure approximately the length of the stem before cutting – you can always cut a little more off but can never add it on! Cut the stems with a slanting cut and hold the stem as near the bottom as possible. Bring the main flowers into the centre of the group and flowing forwards, making sure that the flower heads have a gradual upturn to face you. Daffodils are natural looking flowers and always demand a more casual arrangement: I don't in fact like daffodils used with other flowers, as I always think they look better speaking up for themselves.

If you do the arrangement on a base or tray, it can be completed, say, in the kitchen, and brought in at the last minute. What better than to just pop it on the end of the pasting table; no cloth to wash, just a quick wipe down, and then back to the papering!

Easter Breakfast

Fresh Orange Juice

Boiled Decorated Eggs with Toast Fingers

Hot Cross Buns

Even if there are just two of you on this particular morning, make something of it. Two trays laid up the night before make life easier, but do have masses of daffodils and greenery about (although I mustn't stray too much into Derek's field!). Use your finest glasses for the orange juice, best cutlery for eating the boiled eggs and buttering the hot cross buns. Have your nicest napkins, tablecloth or tray cloth, and have lots of really good coffee or tea. And if you want two or even three of the superb hot cross buns, ruddy well eat them. You can walk off some of the excess weight after lunch!

Fresh Orange Juice

Everybody knows how to extract juice from an orange, so there's not really much for me to say. I must admit I'm not too keen on these new-fangled juice pressing attachments that come with some electric gadgets, as the pressure applied to the half fruit sometimes means that some of the bitter pith is squeezed in too. For me the old-fashioned glass squeezer is the best, but the modern plastic ones are almost as good – particularly the ones that allow you to accumulate your juice in a screw-on compartment underneath.

Depending on the time of year and the type of oranges available, you can use between 2 and 4 oranges per person for fresh juice. Do be generous, as they're so good for you – and after all, for this particular occasion, you're only going to have soft-boiled eggs and hot cross buns to follow.

If feeling in an even more exuberant mood, don't forget that fresh orange juice is lovely as a wake-you-up mixed with equal parts of sparkling white wine. Your day can be started off in truly grand style!

Boiled Eggs

Start your soft-boiled eggs cooking when you sit down to drink your orange juice. Poke them sharply with a needle and put them into a pan of cold water. Bring to the boil and then simmer medium eggs for just over 3 minutes to get exactly the desired runniness of yolk and the white just set.

Make the toast just as the eggs are about ready, spread it quickly with unsalted butter, and cut into fingers which you can dip into the yolk. Wonderful! And do eat the eggs and toast straight away. If you keep the eggs warm, they carry on cooking, and chilly toast is horrible.

Decorated Eggs

Many Easter customs pre-date Christianity, even the name of the festival itself, apparently. Eostre was the Saxon goddess of spring, and the eggs which have become traditional, were sacred to her as a symbol of rebirth.

If you have the time, patience and artistic talent, you can actually paint the raw eggs before you soft-boil them. Ordinary household satin or eggshell vinyl paints (very appropriate) stand up to boiling. You can use white mixed with ordinary water or poster colours, or there are small trial pots of shades available now (a brilliant idea, not just for painting eggs). Use a laundry marking pen for the lettering.

Mostly the eggs that are decorated for Easter – and rolled down hills – are hard-boiled (put eggs into cold water and cook for 8-10 minutes after the water has come to the boil). If you want simpler decorations, use white eggs only, and add to the water before boiling, spinach for a green colour, beetroot or cochineal for a red colour, onion skins wound around for a mottled effect, and narrow strips of masking tape to allow the colour to take on selected parts of the eggs only.

It is easier to work on hard-boiled eggs, so get your artist's smock out, and let your imagination and all that unappreciated talent get to work!

Hot Cross Buns

Makes 24

1¼ lb (550-575 g) strong plain
  flour
1 oz (25 g) fresh yeast
1 tsp caster sugar
½ pt (300 ml) milk, at blood
  temperature
1 tsp each of ground nutmeg,
  cinnamon and salt
2 oz (50 g) caster sugar
2 oz (50 g) each of currants,
  sultanas and chopped candied
  peel
2 oz (50 g) butter, melted
1 large egg, beaten

For decoration

2 oz (50 g) plain flour
¼ pt (150 ml) milk
1 small egg, mixed with ¼ pt
  (150 ml) water and 4 tbsp caster
  sugar for glaze

The cross on hot cross buns may be a relic of the old custom of marking a cross on dough before baking as a charm against evil spirits that might prevent the dough from rising. They can be tricky, I know, but the following recipe has been tried by several delighted friends, who have obviously managed to keep those evil spirits at bay!

What I particularly like about the recipe is that the buns can be started the evening before and left overnight in the refrigerator. They will then rise again in the warmth of your kitchen or airing cupboard when you get up, and will be cooked in 15-20 minutes to be served piping hot for breakfast.

Sieve half the strong plain flour into your mixing bowl. In a small bowl stir the yeast and teaspoon of sugar together to a smooth creamy paste with 2 tablespoons of the warm milk (do not have the milk too hot or you will kill the yeast). When it is nice and frothy stir in the balance of the warm milk.

Pour the milk/yeast mixture onto the sieved flour and mix thoroughly to a nice dough (if using the dough hook of a mixer, it will take about 3 minutes). Cover the bowl with a warm folded tea towel and put in the airing cupboard or somewhere equally warm and draughtproof for 45 minutes.

While the dough is proving, sieve the rest of the flour into a bowl and add the spices, salt, caster sugar, dried fruit and peel, and mix well together to coat the fruit.

After 45 minutes your initial dough should have doubled in size, and into this you now beat the balance of the flour and the fruit. Once again you can use a dough hook or just your hands.

Gradually mix in the melted butter beaten into the egg. Quite quickly you will again have a smooth dough. Cover with the warm tea towel once more and leave for an hour in the same warm, draught-free place.

Turn the dough out onto a board and with a large sharp knife cut off bits the size of small table tennis balls (about 24 in all). With the palm of your hand roll each one into a smooth ball against your working surface. It's quite easy once you get the hang of it; the dough will feel springy, and as you curl your fingers inwards, the circular shape will emerge.

Put the finished buns on a tray lined with greaseproof paper leaving plenty of room for them to rise and spread yet again. At this stage the tray can be put in the refrigerator overnight, covered with clingfilm.

The next morning, take them out and leave to rise for 20 minutes. With a stainless-steel knife, make a cross on the top of each bun. Mix together the flour and milk for the decoration and put in a piping bag. Through a small nozzle pipe thin strands of paste into the cut cross on the bun. Paint the buns all over with the egg, water and sugar glaze and bake for 15-20 minutes in the pre-heated oven at 425°F (220°C), Gas 7.

Easter Breakfast

Throughout the various seasons I mention making your own napkin rings, and once you have grasped this simple idea you can go on for ever and have rings to match any china, season or occasion.

The requirements are the cardboard roll from the centre of cooking foil, kitchen paper, or even loo paper; ribbons; various decorations; scissors; and a tube of glue. I try to use a ribbon about 1½in (3.75cm) wide and I cut my cardboard tube with a sharp knife just slightly less in width.

1. *Measure a piece of ribbon around the diameter of the tube, overlapping about ¼in (6mm), cut and glue the ribbon on.*
2. *Press the ribbon on, with your fingers inside the roll to keep the shape, and glue an appropriate decoration over the join.*

As you can see, it's as simple as could be, so let us go through the year with some ideas.

St Valentine's Day: dark green ribbon, cut-out red hearts.

Easter:	*yellow ribbon, green leaves, small yellow chick.*
Spring:	*pale green ribbon, clusters of small white flowers, green leaves.*
Summer:	*pale pink ribbon, single white linen daisy, a leaf, pale blue ribbon, pink flowers, blue ribbon bows.*
Autumn:	*brown ribbon, selection of tiny dried flowers tied with a bow; or gold ribbon, gold coloured dried Helichrysum flowers.*
Christmas:	*red ribbon, collection of red lacquered berries and leaves; or dark green ribbon, red bow, small gold bells.*

And so it goes on. I usually make a small place card (see page 159) and slip it into the decoration on the napkin holder. I also find that my guests always seem to want to take their napkin holders home with them after the party, which I think is rather nice.

So happy glueing to you all!

Spring Dinner Party

Serves 6

Chilled Avocado and Cucumber Soup with Herb Roly-Polys

Salmon Strips in Greaseproof Paper

Leg of Spring Lamb

Carrot, Turnip, Hazelnut Lettuce Mould

or

Chopped Carrot and Turnip with Black Pepper

Savoury Potatoes

Crème de Menthe Bavarois with Chocolate Leaves

You will have had your friends round for the informal housewarming supper party, but I think you ought to give a more formal party in order to say thank you to both sets of parents.

As far as the actual cooking is concerned, most of the recipes can be prepared well in advance. The soup can be made two days before, the salmon strips can be wrapped in their greaseproof parcels the day before, and the lamb could be marinating in the oil and soy sauce for a day before cooking, or it could be wrapped in its paste the night before. The vegetable mould can be prepared the day before, but the alternative vegetable dish is really a last-minute special. The potatoes can be peeled and left to soak in cold water the night before. The only dish that really needs to be made on the day is the bavarois, although the chocolate leaves too could have been created a day or two before.

Chilled Avocado and Cucumber Soup

Serves 6
3 ripe avocados
½ pt (300 ml) single cream
½ pt (300 ml) natural yoghurt
4 tsp tarragon vinegar
½ cucumber
½ pt (300 ml) cold milk

Halve the avocados and remove the stones. Take out the flesh using a silver spoon, and liquidize with the single cream. Pass through a plastic sieve into a bowl, and stir in the yoghurt and tarragon vinegar.

Peel and deseed the cucumber and then grate coarsely. Fold into the soup and leave to chill.

Just before serving, fold in the cold milk and adjust seasoning. It may need sugar or salt, and sometimes I add the merest touch of horseradish cream. Garnish each bowl with a thin slice of scored cucumber cut into 4 fans, and 3 tiny thin wedges of avocado, with a sprig of parsley in the middle.

Herb Roly-Polys
One thin slice of bought brown wheatmeal sliced loaf will give you from 12 to 15 little rolls. Place slice of bread on a flat surface and, using a rolling pin, stretch it from top to bottom and side to side.

Spread generously with butter, and then squeeze onto this a few drops of lemon juice. Scatter liberally with fresh chopped herbs – mint, parsley, thyme, marjoram, fennel, etc. Cut off the crusts and then roll up into the shape of a cigar and press firmly. Chill.

Using a sharp, serrated, stainless-steel knife, slice off your roly-polys – with care you will easily get 12, and with patience, possibly even 15! Put 4 on the left-hand side of each soup saucer.

Salmon Strips in Greaseproof Paper

Per person
½ oz (15 g) butter, melted
about 4 oz (100-125 g) fresh filleted salmon, cut into chip-size strips
½ lemon
½ tsp each of chopped parsley and mint
1 tbsp white wine
salt and freshly ground black pepper

I like this dish both for its stark simplicity – and for the looks on the faces of those about to eat it, wondering what to do with the bag of greaseproof paper with which they have been presented!

Each portion will need a piece of excellent quality greaseproof paper measuring approximately 8 x 6in (20 x 15cm). Place each piece of paper flat on your working surface and brush with melted butter. Lay the strips of salmon on each, in a diagonal line from top left-hand corner to bottom right-hand corner. Squeeze the lemon on each portion and coat with any remaining butter. Add the parsley, mint, wine, pepper and a little salt. Fold one corner over the salmon to the other corner, making a triangular shape. Fold the two open edges on one side of the triangle together *twice* (little folds of about ¼in or 6mm) and then do the same on the other open edge. Twist the little 'tails' around to hold secure. Put the bags on a baking tray.

Pre-heat oven to 450°F (230°C), Gas 8, and make doubly sure that the oven has reached this temperature before you 'cook' the fish. Make sure your guests are ready to eat the dish, put the baking tray in, and cook for 4 minutes only.

Serve in the paper on piping hot plates and let your guests unwrap their little parcels themselves. The smell is quite tantalizing, and the fish soft, tender and delicious.

Leg of Spring Lamb

A leg of lamb can vary between 3 lb (1.4 kg) and 7 lb (3.1 kg) in weight, and these can serve from 4 to 12 people. A small leg is made up of the leg bone and shank bone, and the larger legs take in the ball-joint and hip bones too – as well as the little tail bone (the delicacy that I, as cook and carver, sneak for myself).

Seldom does one completely finish a whole roast leg of lamb, so there's usually some left over for sandwiches, for eating cold with salads, or for using in other recipes. I clearly recall one dinner party at Brantlea when four of us did, however, finish off a large leg of lamb and we felt not the slightest twinge of guilt afterwards: just utter contentment!

Roast lamb is one of the few dishes that will wait for diners, and will hold its taste and flavour after initial roasting for up to an hour in the warming drawer, covered in foil. But it is best if eaten 20 minutes from the end of cooking time. I give two alternative recipes for roasting lamb, and you can choose which you like.

Crisp Roast Leg of Lamb

Serves 6 at least

1 leg of lamb, about 6 lb (2.7 kg)
6 cloves of garlic, skinned (I have used 12!)
4 tbsp olive oil
4 tbsp soy sauce
1 tbsp sea salt
freshly ground black pepper
4 oz (100-125 g) each of onions and carrots, roughly chopped (save the skins)
parsley stalks
¼ pt (150 ml) Noilly Prat or Dry Martini
¾ pt (425 ml) lamb stock (see method)

The soy sauce is different, and it makes the outside skin crisp. The garlic is a must. You could use a dry Madeira in place of the vermouth.

Make the stock first, with extra bones – the knuckle end and foot for instance – water, onion, and carrot skins and ends, and simmer for at least 1½ hours.

Wipe the lamb dry, then cut each clove of garlic in half (putting the skins into the stock). With the tip of a very sharp knife, make 12 little incisions evenly into and over the leg (if you adore garlic, double this, with a truly pungent result). Push each half clove into these incisions, if necessary using some sort of instrument to shove them further in.

Pre-heat oven to 400°F (200°C), Gas 6. Mix the olive oil and soy sauce together with the sea salt and black pepper in liquidizer until it thickens. Spread as much of this over the lamb as possible, then put it in a roasting tray and cook in the pre-heated oven for 15 minutes. Remove from the oven.

Take leg out, put on side, and scatter the onions, carrots, and parsley stalks on base of pan. Return leg to pan and, having turned oven down to 350°F (180°C), Gas 4, roast for a further 1½ hours. Every 15 minutes or so add any left-over soy/oil mixture and baste the lamb with it. Do remember when taking the roast from the oven to shut the door while you baste, otherwise the heat loss will do the leg no good at all.

When the leg has finished cooking, remove from roasting tin, put into a clean one, cover with foil and return to oven with temperature turned off.

Skim most of the fat from the roasting tin and place what is left over a high flame. Add the vermouth, scraping quickly and roughly all over the surface of the roasting tray in order to get all the meat goodness and juices into the sauce. Pour contents into a saucepan, add the measured amount of strained stock, and simmer over medium heat for 20 minutes. Pass through a sieve and serve as a light accompanying gravy with the lamb. A handful of freshly chopped garden chives scattered over each portion makes a welcome change from mint.

Leg of Lamb Baked in Herbed Flour and Water Paste

This method of cooking lamb is similar to clay-baking, and all the goodness and juices of the lamb are held inside the hardened flour paste. When this is broken, there is the most wonderful aroma.

Get your butcher to chop the knuckle end off the leg to make a neater shape. Wipe the lamb dry. Mix all the remaining ingredients together to a thick paste, and spread over and around the lamb in a baking tray. Make sure it is completely enclosed.

Roast in the pre-heated oven at 475°F (240°C), Gas 9 for 2 hours. Remove from oven and leave standing for 15 minutes. Crack the hard paste with a cleaver or other blunt instrument, and it will crumble off. Carve at once and serve with fresh mint and apple sauce.

Serves at least 6
1 leg of lamb, about 6 lb (2.7 kg)
2 lb (900 g) strong plain flour
4 tsp black pepper
6 tsp salt
6 tbsp chopped fresh herbs
1½ pt (900 ml) cold water

Mint and Apple Sauce

Chop the mint leaves, and mix with the sugar. Add the vinegar and water and the very finely chopped apple.

6 sprigs of fresh mint
1 tbsp caster sugar
2½ fl. oz (75 ml) white wine vinegar
¼ pt (150 ml) water
1 Granny Smith apple, peeled and cored

Chopped Carrot and Turnip with Black Pepper

It is vital for the success of this dish that the carrots and turnips are cut into even-sized shapes about ½in (1.25cm) square. Put vegetables into saucepan, and cover with cold water. Season, place over medium heat and bring to the boil. Simmer swiftly for 8-10 minutes, remove from heat, and drain. Add half the butter to dry saucepan and cook the drained vegetables until the butter has been absorbed.

Remove from heat and turn out onto a board. With a stainless steel kitchen knife, chop merrily away until the carrots and turnips are coarsely chopped. Sprinkle now with a generous amount of pepper, and leave to one side.

When you wish to serve, melt remaining butter per portion in a frying pan, add diced turnips and carrots, and fry for about 3 minutes. Serve immediately. Garnished with a teaspoon of cream from the top of the milk, they are even richer and tastier.

Per person
2 oz (50 g) carrots, peeled, topped and tailed
2 oz (50 g) turnips, peeled, topped and tailed
1 oz (25 g) butter
freshly ground black pepper

Carrot, Turnip, Hazelnut Lettuce Mould

Fills 6 × 3in (7.5cm) ramekins
6 oz (175 g) carrots, peeled
6 oz (175 g) turnips, peeled
1 oz (25 g) butter
3 tbsp double cream
2 tbsp skinned and chopped hazelnuts
3 egg yolks
2 egg whites
good pinch each of onion salt and ground ginger
6 lettuce leaves, blanched

After peeling the carrots and turnips, cut into even, small pieces and put in saucepan of salted water. Bring to the boil and cook with lid on for 15-20 minutes. Remove from heat and drain. Put back into saucepan, add the butter, and simmer for a moment.

Put this mixture into your food processor or blender, and add the cream with the hazelnuts. Whizz around until the mixture is fairly smooth, adding the egg yolks one at a time.

In a separate glass or stainless steel bowl, beat the egg whites until stiff, with the onion salt and ground ginger. Fold the vegetable mixture gently into the stiff egg white. (The moulds can be prepared to this stage the day before.)

Grease and season the ramekins and put a blanched lettuce leaf in the base of each. Portion out the mixture between the ramekins, put into a roasting tray, and pour in boiling water to come half-way up the ramekin sides. Cook in the pre-heated oven at 375°F (190°C), Gas 5 for 15-20 minutes.

If the main course isn't quite ready, turn off the oven and leave moulds for 5 or 10 minutes, and they will come to no harm.

When serving, simply run a sharp serrated knife round the edge of each ramekin, and turn out onto the plate. They look pretty with the cooked lettuce leaf showing at the top.

Savoury Potatoes

Serves 6
2 tbsp bacon fat
6 oz (175 g) bacon, derinded and finely chopped
8 oz (225 g) onions, finely chopped
1/2 tsp dried thyme
1 1/2 lb (675 g) potatoes, peeled and sliced
salt and freshly ground black pepper
1 1/2 pt (900 ml) good chicken stock
melted butter

Fry the bacon in bacon fat, then add the onion. Cook until nice and golden, then add the thyme.

Butter the base and sides of a suitable oven-proof casserole, and start to build the potato slices up in layers. Spread a little of the onion/bacon mixture plus a little of the seasoning between each layer.

Before adding the final layer of potatoes, pour in the chicken stock. Carefully overlap the final layer of slices for a better effect when served, and brush the top with melted butter. Bake at 400°F (200°C), Gas 6 for 1 hour.

Crème de Menthe Bavarois

Put the gelatine in a small saucepan, and in one fell swoop cover with the measured quantities of Crème de Menthe and water. Shake until the gelatine dissolves, and put to one side.

Put the egg yolks in a warm bowl, and start beating with an electric mixer at high speed (make sure that the whisk reaches right down to the base of the bowl). After about 8 minutes start to add the sugar little by little, and it will increase in volume.

Warm the milk in a small pan, along with the vanilla pod, and cool to blood heat. Pass through a plastic sieve a little at a time into the egg/sugar mixture, beating continuously. Remove vanilla pod, and wash and dry pan before returning the milk/sugar/egg mixture to it. Cook over a medium heat, stirring continuously, until the mixture thickens slightly, like a custard for trifle.

Put the saucepan of gelatine and liquid (now solid) over an extremely low heat so that it will slowly reconstitute. Never do this over a high heat or the gelatine will stick to the bottom of the saucepan. Pass through a plastic sieve onto the thick custard and fold together gently and evenly with a long handled spoon.

Put the saucepan somewhere nice and cool (I often put it in the sink and run fresh cold water round it), as you want the warm mixture to cool and begin to set. How long this takes depends very much on the temperature of your kitchen, of course, and it's usually about 20-30 minutes, but whatever you do, don't let it go rock hard, as you have still to fold in the lightly whipped cream.

To give the pud added kick, I usually put a teaspoon of Crème de Menthe in the base of each serving glass. Then I pour in the creamy mixture, cover each glass, and leave to set. Decorate when cold with a twirl of whipped cream and a chocolate leaf.

Chocolate Leaves

I find rose leaves the best. Choose the size you prefer, wipe them with a slightly damp cloth, and leave to dry.

Meanwhile in a small double saucepan, bring together the chocolate and the water, and stir with a wooden spoon until melted. Simply take hold of the stem part of the individual leaf and lay one side of it on the melted chocolate.

Place the leaf, chocolate side up, on a cooling tray and leave to harden. The leaves will peel off their chocolate imprints easily.

Fills 8-10 long-stemmed hock glasses
½ oz (15 g) gelatine
3 tbsp Crème de Menthe
2 tbsp water
4 egg yolks
4 oz (100-125 g) caster sugar
½ pt (300 ml) milk
1 fresh vanilla pod
½ pt (300 ml) double cream, lightly whipped

rose leaves
4 oz (100-125 g) plain cooking chocolate
1 tbsp water

Spring Dinner Party

One of the best ways in which newlyweds can say thank you to their parents for everything is by having them to a meal – and it's such a good way of showing off all those presents!

The flower arrangement should be simple, I think, and the containers need be nothing more than plastic dishes. See the photograph between pages 56 and 57. The soaked floral foam is anchored down with floral foam tape and, when using candles, always place these in first. Do make sure that the candles are well placed and firm – we want no mishaps later (use special holders or cocktail sticks, see page 30).

Start your arrangement by taking your foliage and put five pieces in, low and flowing, like a five-pointed star; never place four pieces in, as you could end up with a square-looking arrangement. Having created this star shape, cut more foliage slightly shorter, and place between your first placements, giving an in-and-out shape. Now insert some foliage nearer to the candles, working around the containers all the time; again, never do one side of the arrangement and think you can repeat it on the other side. It just doesn't work. I used golden privet (Lugustrum vulgare), Cupressus, and separate leaves of laurel (Laurus) for the foliage in these arrangements.

Now, with a good foliage outline, you can follow the same pattern with the flowers. Always cut the stems with a slanting cut, as it gives a point on the end of the stem that is easy to push into the floral foam. Gold roses and gold spray carnations are the flowers for this arrangement, and, as with the foliage, work round the container giving a good all-round effect. Spare pieces of foliage can now be tucked into any empty spaces, covering the mechanics and the floral foam.

Never forget that dinner table arrangements are seen from fairly close up, so do cover up all the works.

I chose the gold colours to pick up the gold edge of the dark green French pottery plates; the dark green linen napkins keep the colouring on the deeper side, and it all looks splendid on a pale green cloth.

Candles
Golden privet
Cupressus
Laurel
Rose
Spray carnation

50

Easter Sunday Lunch
Serves 8

Escalope of Salmon with Spinach Cream Sauce

Butterfly Loin of Lamb with Vegetable Quiche

Coffee Steamed Sponge

Easter Simnel Cake

This should really be a lazy, lying-in-bed morning, but if you organize yourself properly, your lunch will go without a hitch.

You can prepare much of the food the day before; the cake for tea will have been made at least a week before. On the Saturday you can cut the salmon slices, and put them in the fridge with the lemon juice and pepper, covered with clingfilm. The lamb stock could be simmering away all day, you could make the spinach cream sauce, and the vegetable quiche base. The highlight of the meal, though, for me, is the coffee steamed sponge. When you turn it out, the lovely coffee-smelling liquid cascades down the sides of the sponge, and I assure you it works beautifully, and tastes out of this world. It should be prepared and cooked on the day of the lunch.

In my house lunch guests invariably stay on for a cup of tea before departing, so the Simnel cake will just fill up any tiny gap their tummies might well have.

Escalope of Salmon with Spinach Cream Sauce

Serves 8
8 escalopes of salmon
lemon juice
freshly ground black pepper
rosé wine

Spinach cream sauce
1 pt (600 ml) double cream
1 tsp sea salt
spinach purée (see below)

This is a delightful way of cooking salmon at the last minute, and it always impresses guests. It is almost too easy to be true, although there is an element of skill in the initial slicing of the salmon. The best buy from the fishmonger is a whole running fillet of salmon which looks like a side of smoked salmon, and if you are the type of person who can skilfully and smoothly slice the largest, thinnest, most beautiful slivers of salmon off the piece, then you will have no trouble at all. But if you aren't in this superior class, you might have a little difficulty at first.

Using a very sharp knife – stainless steel and serrated – saw backwards and forwards as smoothly as possible to get an escalope of about ¼in (1.25cm) thick, large enough to spread over a serving plate of about 6in (15cm) in diameter. Each escalope should weigh approximately 4 oz (100-125 g) free of skin and bone, so do allow extra for waste when buying.

Make the sauce first. Put the cream into a large saucepan with the salt and simmer away over medium heat until reduced by half. Don't let it boil over. Beat in the spinach purée (with the merest touch of nutmeg if you like), and put to one side in the top of a double saucepan.

When you want to serve, start warming the sauce through gently (it will take about 20 minutes from cold), and place the escalopes on well-buttered baking trays. Season each piece of salmon with a little lemon juice and freshly ground black pepper. Pre-heat the oven well to 450°F (230°C), Gas 8.

Sprinkle some rosé wine over each escalope (just as you would sprinkle vinegar over chip-shop chips) and place the tray in the hot oven. Cook for 3 minutes only. Remove from oven and transfer each escalope on a fish slice to a warmed plate. Coat with the warm spinach cream sauce and serve immediately.

Spinach Purée

1 lb (450 g) fresh spinach leaves
12 oz (350 g) butter
freshly ground black pepper

This rich purée is delicious as a separate vegetable, or is useful in sauce such as that above.

Take the stalks carefully off the leaves. Cut 4 oz (115 g) of the butter into pieces and melt gently in a pan before adding the coarsely chopped leaves. Simmer slowly for 15 minutes, then take off the heat, allow to cool, and liquidize. Pass through a fine plastic sieve, then melt a further 4 oz (115 g) butter and allow the spinach purée to soak this up over a gentle heat. Repeat the cooking process with the third lot of butter and then sprinkle liberally with pepper.

Butterfly Loin of Lamb

You will need a friendly and accommodating butcher to help with this, as you want a saddle of lamb of approximately 4 lb (1.8 kg), but with the loin and rib bones taken out. (Don't let him throw the bones away, as you need them for making the gravy.) The saddle is boned out, leaving both loins joined together and, with the fillets replaced down the middle, each side is rolled inwards and together.

This is then securely tied at 1 in (2.5cm) intervals with fine string. Having paid for this to be done, the actual cooking is easy, the carving even simpler, and the eating divine.

Serves 8
saddle of lamb
4 oz (100-125 g) onions, chopped
4 oz (100-125 g) carrots, chopped
2 stalks celery, chopped
1 clove garlic, crushed
2 sprigs fresh rosemary
4 oz (100-125 g) butter
salt and freshly ground black pepper
2 tbsp plain flour
lamb stock (see method)

The lamb stock for the gravy can be simmering gently away while you do everything else. Put the lamb bones, carrot and onion skins, celery tops, skin off garlic and any other suitable stock ingredients to hand, in a large pan with lots of water to cover, and simmer for as long as you like.

Pre-heat the oven to 450°F (230°C), Gas 8. Gently sauté the chopped vegetables, garlic and rosemary in the butter in a small roasting tin on top of the stove. When browned, turn up the heat, put in the loin of lamb, brown it all over, pressing it down into the hot fat and vegetables with a wooden spoon.

Lightly sprinkle browned joint with salt and pepper, put tin in oven, and cook for 50 minutes. Remove from oven and put the loin on a plate in the warming drawer to 'rest'.

Put the roasting tin on top of the stove over a high heat and add the sieved plain flour. Stir vigorously until browned and then pour on 1 pint (600 ml) of the strained lamb stock. Keep on stirring and cook for about 15 minutes then press through a sieve.

Slice your 'butterflies' and pass the gravy round separately. Serve with a wedge of vegetable quiche.

Vegetable Quiche

Pastry (for an 8-10in or 20-25cm
tin)
8 oz (225 g) plain flour
tiny pinch of salt
1 tbsp icing sugar
5 oz (150 g) softened butter
1 egg, at room temperature

Filling
2 eggs
1 egg yolk
salt and freshly ground black
pepper
pinch of freshly grated nutmeg
½ pt (300 ml) double cream
½ lb (225 g) any vegetable you
have to hand

Make the pastry. Sieve the flour, salt and sugar together, mound onto your working surface, and then make a well in the centre. Place your softened butter into the well, pat the egg into the butter, and then scoop the flour into, over and under the eggy butter. When the texture begins to resemble a shortbread mixture, bring the pastry together with the palms of your hands.

Put it in the bottom of a loose-bottomed flan tin, flour the edges of the tin, and press the pastry lightly to flatten it out over the base and up the sides of the tin. Chill for at least an hour before baking blind (line the tin with foil, fill with dried beans, making sure that the rims are well covered with the foil) for 35 minutes at 325°F (170°C), Gas 3.

Mix together the custard ingredients – the eggs, egg yolk, seasonings and cream. Use literally any vegetable you have: dice carrots, turnips, parsnips or fennel, and blanch for a moment; finely chop onions, mushroom caps or leeks, and sauté lightly in butter; chop peppers or celery. Place your measured weight of prepared vegetables in the quiche base, pour two-thirds of the custard over and bake in oven pre-heated to 375°F (190°C), Gas 5 for 10 minutes. Pull shelf of oven out and cover quiche with remaining custard. Bake for 25 minutes longer.

Coffee Steamed Sponge

Serves 8
Coffee caramel
6 oz (175 g) cube sugar
4 tbsp cold water
2 tbsp instant coffee powder
½ pt (300 ml) warm water

Sponge
2 oz (50 g) soft butter
2 oz (50 g) caster sugar
1 egg, lightly beaten
5 oz (150 g) self-raising flour

Send your guests away with a warm glow in their tummies after this steamed pudding.

First thing in the morning, make the coffee caramel, which is the base of this pudding. Put the cube sugar and cold water into a thick bottomed saucepan and gently dissolve and cook until a rich brown caramelised colour. Meanwhile mix the instant coffee powder with the warm water.

Take great care with the next stage. The heat will be very intense as you pour the coffee mixture onto the caramel, so I suggest you cover your pouring hand with a small towel. Take the caramel from the stove at the last minute, and pour *half, half only,* of the coffee mixture, a little at a time, into the bubbling caramel. Stir with a wooden spoon, and return to the heat and combine well.

Pour into a 1½ pint (900 ml) pudding basin and leave for 3-4 hours. As it cools, from time to time turn and twist the bowl around so that the caramel creeps up the sides of the bowl and sticks tightly.

To make the actual sponge, cream the butter and sugar together until nice and white and fluffy, then slowly beat in the egg with the remaining coffee liquid. If it splits and looks horrible don't panic — it doesn't matter a hoot. Gently fold in the sieved self-raising flour and this will bring the split mixture back together nicely. Pour into the pudding bowl (it only comes about half-way up the sides), cover completely with doubled foil, and tie the over-lapping foil firmly to the outside of the bowl.

Place bowl in a large saucepan and pour in boiling water until it comes half-way up the bowl. Put the lid on the pan and simmer for 1½ hours, topping up with more water if necessary.

The sponge turns out easily, and should be served with a jug of cream.

Easter Simnel Cake

Makes an 8in (20cm) round cake
Marzipan
4 large egg yolks
3 tsp fresh lemon juice
12 oz (350 g) icing sugar, sieved
12 oz (350 g) ground almonds,
sieved

Dried fruit
12 oz (350 g) currants
12 oz (350 g) sultanas
2 oz (50 g) each of candied orange
and lemon peel, chopped
¼ pt (150 ml) Guinness

Cake mix
6 oz (175 g) soft brown sugar
6 oz (175 g) butter
3 fresh medium eggs, lightly
beaten
8 oz (225 g) self-raising flour
½ tsp each of salt, ground nutmeg,
cinnamon and allspice

Apricot glaze
4 tbsp apricot jam
2 tbsp apricot brandy

Being such a staunch traditionalist at heart, I always bake my Simnel cake about 2 weeks before Easter. Allow at least 2 days in which to make it.

Make the marzipan at least a day before you want to use it. Mix all the marzipan ingredients together to a smooth paste. Divide in two, and put in a polythene bag. Leave to rest overnight in the fridge. When you want to use it, bring back to room temperature, and knead it again if you like for a softer, more pliable texture.

The day before mixing and baking the cake, soak the dried fruit ingredients overnight in the Guinness.

When you want to bake the cake, pre-heat oven to 300°F (150°C), Gas 2, and line your tin with a double thickness of the best greaseproof paper available (see page 28). Butter the paper lightly.

Cream the soft brown sugar of the cake mix with the soft butter and then little by little beat in the beaten eggs. Fold in the soaked dried fruit ingredients, and then the flour with the salt, nutmeg, cinnamon and allspice.

Place half the cake mixture into the prepared tin. Roll out half the marzipan to an 8in (20cm) circle, and place on top of the cake mix in the tin. Cover the marzipan circle with the remaining cake mix.

Bake for 3 hours in the pre-heated oven and then remove and test. A thin skewer stuck through the middle should come out clean (bearing in mind that the marzipan in the cake could be slightly soft). If still not cooked, cover with foil and cook for a further 30-45 minutes. Remove and leave to cool.

Meanwhile, prepare the apricot glaze by melting the jam and brandy together gently over a low heat. Paint this all over the cake. Roll out the balance of the marzipan and put on top of the cake. Light the grill and when hot, place the cake under it to brown the top of the marzipan. Decorate as you like, with balls of further marzipan (11 represent the 11 faithful disciples) or with an Easter chick.

A magnificent buffet table for a spring wedding: cold poached salmon, salmon cutlets, French bean salad, fennel salad, Parisian potatoes, stuffed mushroom caps, and red salmon caviare roe hazelnut roulade. The twin flower arrangements in their unusual containers – ashtrays – stand on a boxed table with luxurious ribbon-topped swagging.

Start with the outline of each arrangement, to set
the height and width. The first placement, the spine
piece, of mountain ash, should be as straight and
upright as possible. Place well to the back in the
soaked floral foam, and follow with side-flowing
sprays of the same foliage and sweeps of ivy.

Now fill in the outline of the arrangement. The
autumnal prunus foliage gives depth of colour, as
well as camouflaging the floral foam when
recessed into the centre. The flowing nephrolepis
fern brings movement and texture into the group (it's
this that adds interest).

Flowers that echo the pink berry colour are now introduced. The gladioli follow the spine line of the mountain ash: grade them down in size into the centre of the arrangement. Then place the pink carnations and spray carnations to continue the gentle flow towards the sides.

The centre of any arrangement is the most important, and should hold the 'best', largest or darkest flowers. Pink gerbera are used here, with some small pink roses. Make sure there are no gaps, and the arrangement is now ready to greet your guests.

A simple and eye-catching arrangement for a housewarming party, using old (cleaned) wine bottles, candles, a bunch of daffodils, and fruit.

Opposite. *A table setting for a spring dinner party with low arrangements of gold roses and carnations.*

An unusual decoration for Easter: an Easter egg tree with suspended foil-wrapped eggs and a prolific bird on her nest.

Opposite. *Crème de Menthe bavarois with chocolate leaves for a delicious finale to a spring dinner party.*

*A Simnel cake for an Easter tea,
rich and delicious with its topping
of toasted marzipan.*

*Escalope of salmon with a spinach
cream sauce makes a colourful
and subtle starter for Easter
Sunday lunch.*

Easter Sunday Lunch

Apart from those chocolate eggs that are supposed to be for children (and me), flowers are one of the most important parts of Easter at home. Daffodils, narcissi, etc are all available in profusion around now, so buy or pick them liberally, and arrange simply throughout the house. Their perfume and colours alone tell you that spring is here.

It's the decorative possibilities inherent in Easter images – the egg shapes, the Easter chicks or birds – that I'm interested in. In days of old the custom was to hide eggs around the garden for the children to find, and, if you were clever, you could lose the children all day if the eggs were well enough hidden! You can, of course, organize an indoor egg hunt, but another alternative is to have an Easter egg tree, which looks good, captures the non-religious spirit of the festival, and which children will love! See the photograph between pages 56 and 57.

It's very simple to prepare, but you obviously have to have an interesting branch from which to suspend your eggs. I've used a piece of corkscrew hazel (Corylus avellana contorta or Harry Lauder's Walking Stick), and I've attached it to a base of gnarled driftwood (see what I mean about always being on the lookout for unusual props – I found the driftwood on a river walk one day). Any strong, interestingly shaped branch – perhaps from a hedgerow hawthorn – will do, and the more gnarls and knobs the better to attach the flowers to. You could use a flat container filled with Polyfilla or plaster of paris for the base if you haven't anything suitable, and disguise it with moss and the nest. (See page 156 for further 'tree' ideas.)

Sprays of ivy (hedera) are all that is needed for the foliage at the base of the arrangement, so that the emphasis is put on the eggs. To stop the branch looking too bare, polyester blossom flowers and leaves were glued onto the branch creating a blossoming tree effect.

The small foil-covered chocolate eggs were hung in ribbon hammocks with a long ribbon tail to tie them onto the branch (a little sticky tape will hold the ribbon onto the foil). Hidden in the foliage a bird is keeping its eye on a nest full of eggs – a very busy bird it seems. Try to suggest to the children that the nest can be raided after they've eaten their lunch, but always have a few spare eggs to make up for any stealthy branch losses!

Corkscrew hazel branch and base
Ivy
Polyester blossom flowers and
  leaves
Chocolate eggs
Ribbon

Summer

Fruit

Apples · Apricots · Bilberries · Blackberries · Blackcurrants ·
Blueberries · Cherries · Damsons · Gooseberries · Kiwi fruit ·
Loganberries · Peaches · Plums · Raspberries · Redcurrants ·
Strawberries

Vegetables

Asparagus · Beans (broad, French & runner) · Beetroot · Cabbage ·
Carrots · Courgettes · Cucumbers · *Mange tout* · Marrow ·
Mushrooms (field) · Peas · Peppers · Pumpkin · Red Cabbage ·
Spinach · Sweetcorn · Tomatoes · Turnips · Watercress

Herbs

Basil · Chervil · Chives · Fennel ·Lemon Balm · Lovage · Marjoram ·
Mint · Rosemary · Sage · Savory · Sorrel · Tarragon · Thyme

Summer

Garden and Florist Flowers

Early

Alstroemeria · Arum lily · Gerbera · Peony · Stock · Sweet Pea

Late

Agapanthus (African lily) · Allium · Antirrhinum · Campanula ·
Delphinium · Iris · Larkspur · Lily · Scabious (pincushion flower) ·
Sweet William

All Season Flowers

Carnation (bloom and spray) · Chrysanthemum ·
Gladiolus · Rose

Flowering Shrubs

Azalea · Broom · Deutzia · Lilac (Syringa) · Rhododendron ·
Viburnum · Weigela

Summer Food

I almost wish Mother Nature had been a trifle more considerate, and hadn't given us such a glut of freshness. We are so spoilt, literally, for choice from the beginning of June until the end of August, that it is a season of decisions, decisions, decisions.

Summer for me these days, I suppose, doesn't mean what it does to others: my swimming, sunbathing and relaxing are done in South Africa during the British winter. But I do love British summers, and I associate them primarily with long walks in the early morning, from home to Miller Howe, and with lots of parties and meals eaten outside; I organize picnics and barbecues, candlelit dinners and sumptuous teas. I love those long balmy nights sitting at my summer house watching the sun set over Windermere, with a glass in hand and the promise of delicious food. Often of course – sadly – eating out is spoiled by the caprices of the weather, but you can always eat inside. The food tastes just as good!

Thus we have organized our summer section around all kinds of parties that can be given out of doors: a summer garden party, a children's party, a picnic, a tea party, and Derek's brilliant ideas for transforming a hall or small dining room into a conservatory show how, even if the rain does come pouring down, you can pretend you're in the garden surrounded by greenery!

Although there's such a choice of produce around, I have used chicken as a feature in most of the recipes, and I hope the variety of ideas will open your eyes to chicken's incredible versatility. And the true essence of summer, the soft fruit, I have used in abundance, particularly in the classic British summer pudding.

Summer Flowers

Early summer is such a good time for flowering shrubs and trees and they can be used for outline material in many arrangements. The main thing to remember, though, is that after cutting from the shrub, all the foliage must be stripped off, leaving the blossom. If you think about it, the branches have to work hard to feed the foliage as well as the blossom. All woody stems should have special treatment (see page 12), and it's particularly important in summer when plants are hot and thirsty. I would be even more specific about the timing of cutting: do it in the evening when it's cool, and don't forget the immediate drink before the long overnight drink.

Late on in the summer months many trees and shrubs are very pickable with the mature foliage, which will stand well when cut. Many plants and shrubs are grown by the flower arranger just for the foliage and there are some that no flower arranger would be without. To me, one plant stands head and shoulders above the rest, and that is the Hosta. *There are more than 20 species of this hardy herbaceous perennial, which is a great water lover, and grows well by a stream and in shade. It also makes excellent ground cover and once planted can be left for years. My favourites are:*
*Hosta (*albomarginatea*): green glossy leaves margined white;*
*Hosta (*crispula*): pointed green leaves edged in white;*
*Hosta (*fortunei*): grey-green leaves boldly veined;*
*Hosta (*sieboldiana*): large ovate mid-green leaves, strongly veined.*

I have found that the Hosta grows well in containers and makes a wonderful showy plant when well established. Water every day and use a liquid fertilizer once a week. I have some plants that have been in the same tubs for 10 years and they end up about 4 feet (over 1 metre) across by high summer – and just think of all those leaves!

My other great favourite is Alchemilla mollis, *or Lady's Mantle. Some people think it very invasive but I love it, as even on a dull day the tufts of lime green flowers are such a joy. It is the best arrangement filler-in I know. It can also be put into glycerine later in the year to preserve for the winter months (see page 101).*

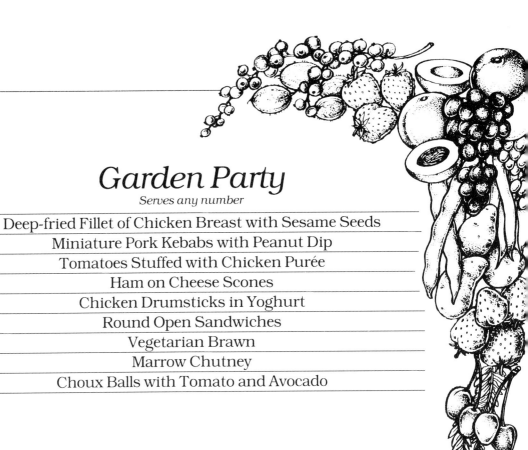

Garden Party

Serves any number

Deep-fried Fillet of Chicken Breast with Sesame Seeds

Miniature Pork Kebabs with Peanut Dip

Tomatoes Stuffed with Chicken Purée

Ham on Cheese Scones

Chicken Drumsticks in Yoghurt

Round Open Sandwiches

Vegetarian Brawn

Marrow Chutney

Choux Balls with Tomato and Avocado

Garden parties aren't just afternoon teas held at Buckingham Palace, but can be lunch, supper or buffet parties for friends and acquaintances, or one prepared by several people on this or that committee in an attempt to raise funds for the cause of their liking.

Once again most of the dishes are prepared way ahead of time and are relatively inexpensive. There is no pudding recipe, as the best thing to serve at this time of year is fresh hulled strawberries with caster or soft brown sugar, and lots of runny double cream!

If the weather is bad, don't be daunted; put the car in the garden and set up the tables in the garage or car port, and just hold the party inside!

Deep-fried Fillet of Chicken Breast with Sesame Seeds

Chicken fillets can be cunningly stored up throughout several months by removing them stealthily from the breasts, and freezing them. When you have a stockpile, and a special occasion, allow to thoroughly defrost, and cook them in the following way.

A chicken fillet is approximately 1½ oz (40 g) in weight, so one will easily cut into 2 good sized mouth-watering portions. Allow 2 fillets (4 pieces) roughly per person.

Shake the pieces in seasoned flour, then dip into beaten egg and roll in sesame seeds. Deep-fry for no more than 3 minutes at 360°F (180°C) and transfer to a baking tray lined with kitchen paper to absorb any surplus fat. Put a small piece of parsley on each one and stick a cocktail stick through the parsley into the fillet (see photograph between pages 80 and 81).

Serves 4
8 chicken fillets
about 1 oz (25 g) seasoned flour
1 egg, beaten lightly
about 2 oz (50 g) sesame seeds
oil for deep frying
parsley sprigs

Miniature Pork Kebabs with Peanut Dip

Buy shoulder of pork (or fillet if feeling extravagant): approximately 1 lb (450 g) of lean meat, with all fat removed, will give you about 20 x 1in (2.5cm) cubes. Allow about 2 cubes per person, depending on what else you put on your kebabs.

Simply toss the cubes in the seasoned flour mixed with your favourite curry powder. Coat the base of a frying pan (about 8in or 20cm in diameter) with cooking oil, heat, and then add 1 oz (25 g) butter. When nice and hot, using a wooden spoon, fry the cubes to seal them, but don't put in more than 10 at a time. To plonk masses in reduces the heat of the fat and oil, and the pork will stew rather than sauté. Cook each batch for 6 minutes only, and clean and replace the oil and fat after cooking 3 batches.

Remove to a tray lined with kitchen paper to drain and when cool make into miniature kebabs on wooden cocktail sticks with cubes of red pepper, onion and aubergine, and stick them into a half orange or melon or similar, for presentation. If you prefer, you can quickly fry the vegetables in a little butter before assembling the kebabs.

The dip for this quantity of meat is made simply by putting the peanut butter into your food processor or blender along with the chopped onion, ginger, cream of coconut, and white wine.

Serves about 10
1 lb (450 g) lean pork
4 oz (100-125 g) seasoned flour
1 tbsp curry powder
oil
butter
2 large red peppers, seeded and
*   cubed*
2 medium onions, cubed
1 small aubergine, cubed

Peanut dip
12 oz (350 g) jar crunchy peanut
*   butter*
4 oz (100-125 g) onion, finely
*   chopped*
pinch ground ginger
2 tbsp tinned cream of coconut
4 tbsp white wine

Tomatoes Stuffed with Chicken Purée

Chicken Purée

1 lb (450 g) cooked chicken flesh
3 oz (75 g) soft butter
1 tbsp double cream
½ tsp nutmeg, grated
1 tsp salt
juice of ½ lemon
1 tbsp finely chopped chives

To get the right effect here you really do want to have the smallest tomatoes possible, so that each filled tomato can be popped into the mouth like an old-fashioned gobstopper. Cut the top off with a sharp knife and take out the core and seeds with a teaspoon.

It is often quite difficult, though, to find really small tomatoes, so tomato halves can be used. Remember to slice the tomato through the middle across the equator, and not through the middle of the stalk bit. Cut away the centre cores and seeds, and then you can pipe the mixture into the tomato half.

Allow about 2-3 tomatoes per person. 1 lb (450 g) of cooked chicken flesh will easily fill 32-40 tomatoes.

Blend all the ingredients together in the food processor or blender until smooth. Leave for about 30 minutes to rest, then it will be easier to pipe into the tomatoes.

Ham on Cheese Scones

Cheese Scones

1 lb (450 g) self-raising flour
6 oz (175 g) very soft butter
pinch of salt
4-5 oz (125-150 g) Cheddar cheese, grated
ground coriander or curry powder to taste
2 eggs, lightly beaten
milk or sour cream, to mix

This is a very simple – and rather homely – open sandwich. You can buy some cooked ham, of course, but it's much better to cook and use your own (see page 94). This quantity of scone dough will make about 20 scones, which you then split; you could double the quantities and freeze some. You'll need about 1½ lb (700 g) of ham for this quantity of scone halves. Allow 2 per person.

To make the scones, pre-heat the oven to 425°F (220°C), Gas 7. Sieve the flour into a large bowl, and break the butter up into pieces into the bowl. Mix flour and butter together with your fingers until it starts to come together and resemble fine crumbs. Add the salt, cheese, seasoning and eggs, and start to bring together. Do not squeeze.

Mix in milk or sour cream modestly until the mixture is just right – not too soft nor too dry (it all depends on so many factors) – and then turn out onto a floured board. Pat out to about 1in (2.5cm) thick and cut into squares. Put on trays and bake for about 15 minutes. You could top with a little extra grated cheese if you like.

When generously buttering the cold split scones, add the merest touch of mustard to the butter. Cut largish slivers off the ham quite thinly so that they can be folded into a squashed 'S' shape, which makes a generous topping. A touch of your favourite chutney on top of the ham adds taste (see page 67), and sprinkle the lot finally with finely chopped parsley.

Chicken Drumsticks in Yoghurt

I was recently asked to submit an unusual 2-course family meal for 4 which was to be economical, tempting, filling and simple. When I asked how economical was economical, I nearly passed out when they specified 2 substantial courses with at least 4 vegetables for £1 per person!

Now I know I'm a dab hand at throwing dishes together with the oddest and most interesting combinations, but I rebelled at all that for 4 for £4. The staff told me I needed to come down out of the clouds, so I did just that, and decided to prepare this dish with 3 vegetables, a tasty potato dish, and to end with an ice-box pudding.

When D-Day came, I had to submit my recipe plans. The BBC calculator was put to work as I reeled off the ingredients. Tension mounted, eyebrows were raised at the very mention of double cream, but when it was all added up, audited and double checked, it came to only £4.08! So, as you can see, this is an economical, as well as delicious, dish (see photograph between pages 80 and 81).

Marinate the drumsticks in the yoghurt in a flat dish for 3 days, turning in the morning and evening to make sure each drumstick is coated all over.

You then coat the drumsticks with whichever coating you choose, turning and pressing, until thoroughly encased. Return to the yoghurt dish.

Pre-heat the oven to 375°F (190°C), Gas 5, and put dish in oven. Bake for 30 minutes. Turn oven up to 425°F (220°C), Gas 7, and cook for a further 30 minutes (turn the drumsticks if you like). Serve immediately, or leave to get cold, when the drumsticks taste equally delicious.

Per 4 drumsticks

4 drumsticks, weighing about 5 oz (150 g) each
½ pt (300 ml) natural yoghurt

Coatings

1. *2 oz (50 g) crushed cornflakes, with the merest touch of curry powder*
2. *3 oz (75 g) desiccated coconut*
3. *2 oz (50 g) fine white, stale breadcrumbs mixed with 1 oz (25 g) grated Cheddar cheese, 2 cloves finely crushed garlic and 1 tbsp chopped parsley*

Round Open Sandwiches

Bought brown sliced bread (preferably with a little wheatmeal in it) is the best for these, but you will need a very sharp round fluted cutter of about 2in (5cm) in diameter. If your slice of bread is about 4 × 4in (10 × 10cm), this size cutter will allow you to get 3 rounds out of each slice (and a loaf usually contains about 26 slices). Although it sounds wasteful it is much quicker to butter the whole slices of bread before cutting out the rounds, which ensures that the butter is beautifully spread right up to the very edges of your circles.

The merest touch of fresh lemon juice and rind in your soft butter adds to the taste and when making lots of sandwiches I usually let the butter get soft and then whip in my flavouring with an electric hand whisk. This means the butter is lovely and creamy and so, so easy to spread. Do butter your bread generously; it not only adds taste (and luxury), but the butter prevents the filling soaking through to bread, making it soggy.

Toppings

Very, very thin slices of cucumber (remember to score it first) and then a slice of cold hard-boiled egg, topped off with a dab of mayonnaise and a parsley leaf.

A slice of kiwi fruit topped off with a piped twirl of cream cheese looks attractive surrounded with the thinnest slices of radish.

Cold scrambled eggs (page 155) are ideal for using on this type of sandwich, and can be varied in flavour with tomato purée, horse-radish cream, chives, smoked salmon bits, minced ham, etc.

Cooked or canned prawns and shrimps are delicious when placed on top of a twirl of cream cheese.

All sorts of pâtés and cold meats like tongue are ideal.

Peanut butter with a slice of tomato topped with pickled onion, and surrounded by gherkin slices.

Garnishes

Always garnish your sandwiches, using any of the following: with capers, criss-cross anchovies, stuffed olive slices, diamonds of red pepper, grated cheese, halved and seeded grapes, spring onion bits, chopped raw onion, walnut or pecan halves, red or black lumpfish roe, apple sauce, kumquat slices, etc (see the photograph between pages 80 and 81 for some further ideas).

You can prepare the sandwiches early in the day provided you place them on the serving dishes lined with slightly damp lettuce (please, not swimming in water, as the sandwiches will end up sticking to the roof of your mouth!). Cover with clingfilm and leave in a cool place.

Vegetarian Brawn

Vegetarians celebrate too, and often at buffets can find lots of rabbit food to eat, but it takes more than that to fill the average belly! Boiled eggs might be allowed, and chunks of cheese, but this 'brawn' is delicious, with a taste of curry powder (which can be substituted with tomato paste if preferred). We used to prepare this when I was in Nyasaland years ago, when what meat there was available was often highly suspect.

This will fill either a 2 lb (900 g) loaf tin or a large Christmas pudding bowl – nicer turned out of the latter, as you can then serve in wedges.

Put the macaroni into a saucepan, cover with cold water and add the salt. Bring up to the boil and simmer for 10 minutes, then strain and refresh under cold running water. Cut into ½ inch (1.25cm) pieces.

Meanwhile simmer the finely chopped onion in the milk until soft, and then add the grated cheese and chopped tomatoes. Mix well.

Mix the Farola or semolina to a paste with the sherry, then add to the milk mixture and bring back to the boil. Remove from the heat and fold in the 2 beaten eggs, the chopped hard-boiled eggs, sage, parsley, curry powder, petits pois and macaroni. Mix well, turn into the greased tin or bowl, and weight down if you like. When cold, chill and turn out and slice.

Serves 8

1 lb (450 g) short-cut macaroni
2 tsp salt
4 oz (100-125g) onions, finely chopped
½ pt (300 ml) milk
4 oz (100-125 g) Cheddar cheese, grated
¾ lb (350 g) tomatoes, skinned, seeded and finely chopped
2 oz (50 g) Farola or semolina
2 tbsp sherry
2 raw eggs, beaten
6 hard-boiled eggs, chopped
1 tbsp finely chopped fresh sage
1 tbsp finely chopped fresh parsley
1 dessertsp curry powder
4 oz (100-125 g) defrosted frozen petits pois

Marrow Chutney

A much maligned vegetable, which seems to grow in profusion when people take the trouble to plant it, is marrow. At Miller Howe ours are delivered twice weekly by a local smallholder, who supplies us with various delicacies during the summer. Mrs Wild sends us so many, we had to invent a way of using them, and now our marrow chutney is used often and enthusiastically as a garnish to starter dishes.

Simply place all the ingredients into a clean, thick-bottomed saucepan and simmer for 1 hour, stirring from time to time. When cold, pot in sterilized jars.

Fills 5 x 1 lb (450 g) jars

3 lb (1.35 kg) marrow, peeled and evenly chopped into ½in (1.25cm) cubes
4 oz (100-125 g) raisins
1 large onion, finely chopped
¾ lb (350 g) demerara sugar
½ oz (15 g) ground ginger
pinch of salt
1 pt (600 ml) malt vinegar

Choux Balls with Tomato and Avocado

Makes 30

7½ fl. oz (200 ml) water
2½ oz (65 g) butter
3¾ oz (scant 100 g) well sieved
  strong plain flour
pinch of salt
3 eggs, lightly beaten

Filling

3 avocados, skinned, stone
  removed
8 ripe tomatoes, skinned and
  seeded
1 lb (450 g) cream cheese

Pre-heat the oven to 400°F (200°C), Gas 6, and have some baking trays, a piping bag, and a ¼in (6mm) plain nozzle to hand. Heat the water and butter together in a saucepan over a low heat and when the butter has melted, turn up the heat and add the flour and salt all in one go. With a wooden spoon, beat everything thoroughly together for 1 minute over a reduced heat, until it comes together, and leaves the sides of the pan.

Leave to get cold. Using your mixer or merely your hand and a wooden spoon, add the eggs very slowly to the paste, beating all the while, and never adding more until the last addition has been thoroughly absorbed. When all the egg has been added, beat vigorously for 1 minute until it is a shiny gold, and then spoon into the piping bag. Dampen the baking trays and pipe small balls onto them – you should get about 30, allowing about 2 per person. Put the choux balls into the oven and turn up the heat immediately to 425°F (220°C), Gas 7. Cook for about 10-15 minutes or until well risen and golden. These balls need to be very well cooked initially so that they are quite crisp. Turn off oven and leave to cool in oven.

Slice the top off each ball and scoop out any soggy pastry in the middle with a teaspoon.

To make the filling, liquidize the avocado flesh with the tomatoes, and fold this rather runny mixture into the cream cheese. Spoon into the piping bag and pipe into the balls, finishing off with a regal twirl on the top. A thin slice of stuffed olive or a mint leaf is a simple garnish.

You could fill the choux balls with other savoury fillings – with a salmon mousse, with a cheese and herb pâté, etc. Use your imagination . . . and look at the photograph between pages 80 and 81.

Garden Party

Summer is probably the time of the year that all of us look forward to most – to summer and sunshine, of which we always get too little. But, assuming we have good weather, one sure way of getting into the summer mood is to arrange a garden party. You don't have to have a beautifully landscaped garden or patio-edged pool, as any outdoor area offers scope.

Basketry has always been a great favourite medium of mine. The first baskets were made by primitive people for storing grain and foods, and for transporting them from place to place. Gradually baskets were made for other purposes. In the Middle Ages baskets were filled with flowers and hung on doors at festival time – which could have been the start of flower arranging! Simple basketry of good proportion and natural beauty seems to have an affinity with plant materials, and although it is true that in general baskets are rather informal, as in all things it's a matter of degree. There are no rules; you can be as free as you like, but above all remember that the basketry is part of your design and it must be seen. Just because you got a lot for a little does not mean that you don't have to show it off. Also, as basketry is generally of a natural colour, it makes it easy to use any and all flower colours. I have used baskets in every season, including Christmas. The only fault I can find about collecting baskets is where to keep them! Baskets, trays and platters are always useful for either a base or to stand behind an arrangement, round fat shapes can either be containers or can spill out of the front of an arrangement as an accessory.

For an out-of-doors buffet party such as this, a tall basket structure as in the drawing is ideal. It is a five-tiered basket given extra lift on an upturned waste-paper basket. Using a container like this, you have something rather spectacular which will be noticed. I would not want to hide the interest of the basket completely, so I would keep the flower groups in 3 areas only, as shown. Wire plastic containers holding soaked floral foam onto the basket in the 3 chosen positions. Place the outline foliage material in first and work on all 3 groups at once so that the tiered basket is treated as a whole.

I would use the lovely shaped foliage sprays of the shrub Escallonia, a most useful shrub for both the foliage and the delightful blossom – which ranges from pale pink, Escallonia ('Apple Blossom'), to a deep carmine in colour, Escallonia ('Glory of Donard'). Carnation sprays in pale pink could be the first flower placements; these are such useful flowers because the spray is made up of both buds and full open flowers.

Place the carnation sprays in all 3 areas followed by full size pale pink carnations, gradually bringing the large flowers towards the centre. Now recess a little larger and bolder foliage –

ivy (hedera), say — to cover the plastic container and floral foam. The final flowers to be placed could be some lovely summer roses of a slightly deeper pink. Grade the flowers in size from the outside towards the centre and also in colour from pale to deep.

Use the spaces left over for small open sandwiches or whatever. As baskets were used first for food and then for flowers, what better than the combination here, of both food and flowers.

You can get tiered effects using other types of containers, not just basketry. I particularly like the dramatic look of the tiers, and have used a metal kitchen pan stand on occasions. Most of these stands have 5 shelves or ledges. Fix plastic containers on the top and every other ledge, to hold the floral foam blocks, and go for the same sort of shape as I have in the tiered baskets. I once used a pair of white metal pan stands on a summer buffet, with nothing but wild Queen Anne's Lace, Lady's Mantle (Alchemilla mollis) and a few sprays of ivy (hedera), and the effect was super: not one person noticed the lowly origins of the container!

Another container idea that gives a tiered effect is a glass cake stand. These were very popular about 30 years ago for afternoon tea cakes, but then started turning up at jumble sales. Now they are much sought after again, but can still be found reasonably cheaply. Place floral foam and arrange the flowers as described for both the baskets and the pan stand. I have a set of 5 glass stands in my kitchen, which hold the week's supply of fruit and vegetables — and very effective they look too.

Summer Dinner Party
Serves 8

Savoury Ham Peach

Summer Salad Soup

Cardamom Chicken with Hazelnut and Carrot Cream

Summer Pudding

I am certainly one for capturing a little magic on the odd occasion even if it may mean a little extra effort. Derek's garden room effect is stunning, but I actually tested this informal dinner party meal in my summer house at the top of the sloping garden — and the top is quite a long way from the back door up a tricky flight of not-too-firm steps. I had to spend a couple of hours tidying the little house, then we just managed to move in the outdoor wood benches and table that are used when I barbecue on the sun patio, and it was a bit of a squeeze, but oh, on the night it was magic. I lit some nightlight outdoor candles, which give plenty of subdued light and also a bit of warmth on an English 'summer's' evening; the lake in the distance was as calm as a millpond, the hills on the horizon were so clear and the sky was beautifully lit with stars and moon. I didn't mind at all hauling the food up those rickety steps but I must admit I left all the dirties stacked up round the corner for the next day!

It was when the summer pudding was served that the party came into its own. This is such a special pudding to serve. If I go out to South Africa to see my friends in July or August I take them out basins of summer pudding as a gift. Occasionally the Customs men are suspicious and can't understand this madman taking stewed (!) fruit from England to the fruitful winter in South Africa.

Savoury Ham Peach

Serves 8

8 ripe, firm peaches
12 oz (350 g) cooked ham
3 oz (75 g) cream cheese
1 tbsp finely chopped parsley
1 tsp mustard
1 tsp redcurrant jelly
8 shelled walnuts, finely chopped
2 egg whites, beaten stiff

Place 10 oz (275 g) of the ham, the cheese, parsley, mustard and jelly into your food processor or blender and mix to a creamy consistency. Remove to a bowl, and fold in the walnuts followed by the stiffly beaten egg whites.

Place the peaches on your work surface; stem side down, and slice off each top about 1 in (1.25cm) down. (You could vandyke the top instead if you like.) Using a grapefruit knife, slowly and carefully work your knife up and down around the stone. The easiest way of removing the loosened stone is to ease the prongs of an old fashioned carving fork down each side of the stone. The two prongs will tighten round the stone and after a little jiggling, you should be able to take the stone out – rather like a dentist removing a tooth!

Pipe the creamy mixture into each peach, filling it to the top, and if you use a star nozzle, finish off with a twirl on the top, and a snip of parsley. Cut the remaining ham into thin long chip-like shapes, and drape over the edge of the peach for a stunning effect. Serve nestling in crisp lettuce leaves in a bowl, or on a bed of shredded lettuce on a small plate.

Summer Salad Soup

Serves 8

16 radishes
8 spring onions
2 hard-boiled eggs
4 tomatoes
¼ cucumber
1 avocado
1 clove garlic, crushed with 1 tsp
*   salt*
¾ pt (425 ml) natural yoghurt
¾ pt (425 ml) single cream
1 tbsp tarragon or white wine
*   vinegar*
2 oz (50 g) Cheddar cheese, finely
*   grated*
1½ tbsp chopped parsley or
*   chopped mixed seasonal herbs*

This soup should always be served well chilled, in chilled bowls.

Chop the radishes, spring onions and hard-boiled eggs finely. Skin and pip the tomatoes, then chop finely. Peel and remove seeds from cucumber and chop finely. Remove skin and stone from avocado and chop the flesh finely.

Crush the clove of garlic with the salt and combine with the yoghurt, cream and vinegar, then fold in all the chopped vegetables and eggs, and leave to chill.

Serve garnished with the grated Cheddar cheese and chopped herbs.

Cardamom Chicken with Hazelnut and Carrot Cream

Place the marinade ingredients in a liquidizer or food processor and blend until the cardamom seeds are powdered. Dry the chickens well and put ½ skinned onion and 1 carrot inside the ribcage of each.

Coat the chickens liberally with the marinade and then place each into a large strong plastic bag, spooning the balance of the marinade in too. Secure tightly with a bag tie and leave for at least 36 hours, turning from time to time.

Pre-heat oven to 400°F (200°C), Gas 6. Remove chickens from bags and place in roasting tin breast down. Pour over any remaining marinade and cook for 1½ hours, turning the chickens round one quarter every 15 minutes, and basting. When cooked, leave for a few minutes, and then divide each chicken into 4 portions.

Reduce the cream for the hazelnut and carrot cream by half (gently), and then beat in the ground hazelnuts and finely grated carrots. Spoon this onto the individual plates and place the chicken portion on top. Garnish each plate with a sprig of parsley.

Serve the chicken with a delicious green salad, tossed in a walnut dressing (see page 93).

Serves 8
2 fresh chickens, about 3½ lb (1.5 kg) each
1 medium onion, halved
2 carrots, peeled

Marinade
1 pt (600 ml) natural yoghurt
2 tsp cardamom seeds (casing removed)
2 tbsp finely grated fresh root ginger
8 cloves garlic, skinned and chopped finely
2 tsp salt
½ tsp cayenne pepper

Hazelnut and Carrot Cream
1 pt (600 ml) double cream
4 oz (100-125 g) ground hazelnuts
2 carrots, finely grated

Summer Pudding

Serves 8

8 oz (225 g) strawberries, hulled
8 oz (225 g) raspberries, hulled
4 oz (100-125 g) redcurrants,
   destalked
4 oz (100-125 g) blackcurrants,
   destalked
4 oz (100-125 g) gooseberries,
   topped and tailed
4 oz (100-125 g) apples, peeled,
   cored and finely sliced
6 oz (175 g) caster sugar
soft butter, to grease basin
about 8 medium slices white
   bread, without crusts

Nearly everybody has their own version of summer pudding, and I must admit to liking every single one I have ever eaten! This is my version.

Wash and pick over the fruit, and if the strawberries are very large, cut them in half lengthwise. It's fiddly getting the currants off their stalks, but this can be relatively simple if you hold the thick part of the stem firmly between your thumb and first finger, and then run the top part of the prongs of a silver fork quickly along the stem to pull the berries off.

Place all the fruits with the sugar into a large saucepan over a very gentle heat and cook for 5 minutes – or for a shorter time if the sugar has melted and the juices have already begun to run. (Many people go wrong at this stage and cook the fruit for far too long, ending up with a gooey mess minus the individual flavours.) Remove from the heat and set to one side.

Lightly grease all over inside a 1½ pt (900 ml) pudding basin with soft butter and sprinkle with a little caster sugar. Line the basin with the bread slices, making sure you overlap cleverly and leave no gaps – otherwise the juice will find these gaps and make a mess of your pud. (As you have greased the sides of the bowl, the bread will stick readily, but you will have to use a bit of pressure.)

Pour the partly cooked fruit into the well of bread, and then top off the pudding with a further slice or two of bread. Place a saucer or plate that will just fit snugly inside the bowl on top of the pudding, and weight it down with a heavy tin or jar, or a couple of large bags of sugar. Leave in the refrigerator for at least 24 hours before attempting to serve.

When you wish to serve, remove the weight and saucer, and gently press down right round the top rim of the pud to allow a little air to get round the sides. Place your serving dish face down on top of the bowl and then quickly turn over. The pudding should flop out easily. Cut into 8 wedges after proudly presenting the pudding to your guests, and serve simply with lightly whipped double cream.

You *could* keep back some of the fruit juice to colour any outside of the pudding that hasn't turned red, but I quite like to see the odd patches of white.

Summer Dinner Party

Those lucky enough to have a garden room or conservatory have the ideal location for an informal summer dinner party. If you haven't got such a room, however, you can create that effect quite easily, and it's amazing how summery and different it can make your dinner party. It will require a bit of shifting around of furniture, perhaps, and certainly demands a gathering together of all your house plants. If your dining room or kitchen wouldn't suit, why not think about using the hall? Many aren't big enough for a chair, but some would take a round table to seat 4 or 6, and look stunning dressed up as a garden room.

The first thing to give thought to is colour, and as there is now a profusion of green plants in our garden room, we must work around green (it may be considered unlucky, but how can you be a flower arranger and not use green?). The white painted garden furniture in the garden room photograph between pages 80 and 81 is a wonderful complement to the tropical greenery; there's green again for the table covering, and white china finishes the effect. White flowers are called for, and the daisy shapes spell summer straightaway.

At the foot of the arrangement is a green hessian-covered base (see below) and the main feature is the pair of Italian candle galleries. One stands slightly higher than the other (merely because I think it looks better), which I raised on a straight-sided tin covered in the same green hessian. As the round bases of the glass candle galleries take up quite a large amount of space on the base, I decided that an oblong-shaped container for the floral foam would sit much better between them. Whenever using feature objects like these candle galleries, always get them into position first and build the arrangement around and to them.

As some of my plants in the grouping are my ever favourite ladder ferns (Nephrolepis), I sneaked some pieces off as part of the outline of the arrangement together with fine sprays of a green Berberis. I started by placing in the first high straight piece of fern between the galleries and then the same foliage, flowing down towards the base, was placed, almost horizontally, into the floral foam. Thicken this outline by secondary but slightly shorter placements of the same plant material. Introduce some of the fine sprays of Berberis following the lines already created with the ferns. Now introduce the green grapes flowing across the arrangement and cascading over the foot of the glass galleries, to soften the hard line (always cut the grape bunches into smaller bunches, as they can be arranged back into one that has a better shape). Now at this stage, having been working from both sides of the floral foam container, you should be getting some idea of how the finished arrangement is going to look. Notice that you

Candle galleries
Nephrolepis fern
Berberis
Grapes
Roses ('Tiara')
Spray chrysanthemum ('Bonnie
  Jean')
Ivy

come down from the top piece of foliage fairly steeply, not fanning the flowers out.

As always for table arrangements, don't have the individual flowers too large — I think the shorter you cut large flowers the larger they seem to become! I started at the top again by placing in 3 white 'Tiara' roses cut to 3 different lengths to give that gradated effect, then I went to the sides and then, low down near the base, I placed 2 more roses coming in almost at right angles. (When cutting roses, strip off most of their foliage as the moisture will then go straight to the flower and it will last longer.)

White Bonnie Jean spray chrysanthemums were my next flowers (such a useful flower, the spray chrysanthemum, and Bonnie Jean's single daisy shape looks good in the summer and lasts so well). These daisy-shaped flowers should be used on single stems, bringing together the top part of the arrangement with the sides. Now the arrangement should look like a long drawn out pyramid. Before placing in the last of the 'Tiara' roses recess into the centre some foliage to tidy up this area, to give weight and to hide the floral foam. I have used some medium sized ivy leaves (hedera canariensis) on short stalks and recessed. The final flower placements are the flowers to take away any flatness, used on stems so that they stand proud of the other flowers, introducing a three-dimensional effect.

Have one final look at the arrangement all round, making sure that you have no gaps and that all the floral foam is hidden.

Covered Bases

Many flower arrangements look good with a base underneath; which acts as a frame for a picture, to hold everything together. The green hessian base here, and many others I use elsewhere throughout the book, are very easy to make. All you need is fibreboard, fabric for covering, glue, pins, and braid for the sides.

Simply cut shapes out of fibreboard — round, square, oblong, diamonds, etc. Choose your covering fabric, press it if necessary and cut it to size, slightly larger than the board. Don't put any glue on the top surface of the board, but apply a coating of glue around the side edges only. Most glues dry quickly and also can seep into the fibreboard, so let the first coat dry and then apply another. Place the fabric over the top of the board, and pull the fabric onto the glue. (You don't apply glue to the top surface because of glue seepage and so that you can pull the fabric onto the glue, pulling out any creases and tucks.) Push a straight dressmaker's pin through the fabric into the fibreboard edge. Work around the base pushing a pin in about every 4in (10cm).

Once you have finished pulling and pinning, turn the base over and trim off the surplus fabric giving a good straight edge. Finish off by glueing on some matching or contrasting braid; this covers all the pin heads and makes a neat finish.

Children's Party
Serves 8 upwards (depending on age and appetite!)

| Spicy Chicken Wings |
| Spare Ribs |
| Dips |
| Cheese Straws |
| Chicken Rolls |
| Stuffed Tongue Rolls |
| Face Sponge Cake |
| Green Jelly Field Mice |
| Ice Cream Clowns |

I like to spoil kids silly for a relatively short period once or twice a year and that is my bellyful for the 365 days! Not being a family man myself, my first instincts are to give friends' children a pound and send them down to the village for the junk food they seem to appreciate.

In my childhood, party teas consisted of blancmanges, jellies, trifles, cream cakes and masses of sandwiches – banana and honey, egg and cress, and, the treat of treats, canned salmon. These days, however, kids seem to like savouries more, and most of the following recipes will be enjoyed by both adults and children alike. I was amazed when we had a 'testing' party that the kids enjoyed playing games of my childhood, updated a little, and then, as soon as the word was given that they could eat, eat they ruddy well did! The little girls seemed to take a wicked delight in biting the heads off the pear mice and the boys' eyes glistened as they ate the clowns' eyes from the ice cream cornets! Or was it my imagination?

Spicy Chicken Wings

32 chicken winglets
4 oz (100-125 g) butter
½ pt (300 ml) tomato ketchup
¾ pt (425 ml) soy sauce
2 tsp English mustard
4 tsp soft brown sugar
¼ pt (150 ml) pineapple or orange
* juice (or cider)*
2 tbsp Worcestershire sauce
salt and freshly ground black
* pepper*

The most economical thing to buy is chicken winglets, which are available in some good supermarkets. But if you can't get hold of them, every time you buy a chicken clip off the winglets and pop them in the freezer. When you have enough, make this recipe – the sauce would also enhance any other cut of chicken. You can use fewer winglets, but they haven't much meat on them – and they tell me that parents coming to collect their offspring are pretty good at finishing up things ...

Melt the butter in a large frying pan or roasting tin, and fry the wings, using a wooden spoon to occasionally press them down, sizzling, into the hot butter. Fry and turn for about 15 minutes, and then strain off the fat.

Meanwhile mix all the other ingredients together in a bowl and put into the frying pan. Stir mixture together, bring to the boil, then simmer gently for 10 minutes until it reduces and thickens and clings to the winglets.

Have plenty of paper tissues or paper napkins to hand (or better still, damp cloths), as the wings are messy to eat – but oh so good.

Spare Ribs

2 lb (900 g) Chinese spare ribs (in
* racks)*
¼ tsp chilli powder
¼ pt (150 ml) tomato juice
¼ pt (150 ml) pineapple juice
1 tbsp soy sauce
1 tbsp English mustard
1 tsp Worcestershire sauce
1 tsp runny honey
1 tsp salt
1 tsp tomato purée
¼ tsp cayenne pepper
about ¾ pt (425 ml) chicken stock

This recipe makes a particularly rich thick sauce.

Blend all the marinade ingredients (except the stock) in a liquidizer and leave the whole racks of spare ribs in this for at least 24 hours. Divide into individual ribs.

Place the lightly coated ribs in a buttered roasting tray and bake in the oven for 30 minutes at 450°F (230°C), Gas 8, and then add half the remaining marinade. Cook for a further half hour and repeat with the last of the marinade, cooking for a further 20 minutes. The pan will turn quite sticky and brown, so if needed, each time you add some marinade, add some of the chicken stock.

Serve at once, giving your guests large napkins, with plenty of finger bowls around! This dish could also be a very messy supper starter.

Dips

Once the kids have started to get themselves all clarted up with the chicken wings and ribs, you might as well accept the mess and let them loose on lots of different dips, using potato crisps or cheese straws as the scoops. More sophisticated party people use little bits of dry toast, small wheat biscuits, crudités or cooked meat or sausages, but crisps are perennially popular with the more youthful among us.

Dips require only a little imagination, are fun to eat, and are good tummy fillers. Sour cream or cream cheese makes the ideal base, either separate or mixed together, and then you add any of the following to taste: chives, herbs, curry powder, paprika, horseradish, Cheddar and Roquefort cheeses, mustard (powdered or mixed), Worcestershire sauce, mayonnaise, chopped onions, toasted sunflower seeds, garlic, anchovy fillets, tinned chopped water chestnuts, fresh ginger, preserved ginger, tuna fish, avocado, soft-boiled eggs, lumpfish roe. Try to vary the colours of the dips – the more colours, the better...

Dollop out into small soup bowls for the party participants to go wild on.

Cheese Straws

Sift together the flour and seasoning, and rub in the butter until the texture is crumbly. Add the cheese, mix well, and stir in enough beaten egg to make a rough dough.

Knead the dough on a lightly floured board until smooth, and then roll out to about ¼in (6mm) thickness.

The nicest way of serving them is in bundles, and kids love unusual things like long biscuits. Cut out about 15 circles with a 1½in (3.5cm) cutter, and then cut out the centre portion with a smaller cutter (or tiny glass) to make a Polo-mint shape. Cut the rest of the dough into long straws, re-rolling if necessary. Place the circles and straws on greased baking sheets and bake in a pre-heated oven set at 400°F (200°C), Gas 6 for 8-10 minutes until golden. Cool on a wire tray and store in airtight tins. When serving, push as many straws as you can through the circles, and offer in bundles.

You could also use frozen shortcrust or puff pastry for these.

8 oz (225 g) plain flour
celery salt and pepper
4 oz (100-125 g) butter
5 oz (150 g) Cheddar cheese,
  finely grated
1 egg, lightly beaten

Chicken Rolls

Makes 40 × 2in (5cm) rolls
1 lb (450 g) puff pastry
12 oz (350 g) cooked chicken, minced
1 medium onion, grated
pinch of curry powder
½ tsp salt
2 tbsp cooked rice
1 egg, beaten with 1 tbsp milk, for wash

Divide the pastry into 4 parts, then roll out, part by part, into oblongs measuring 20 × 4in (50 × 10cm) approximately. Mix the chicken, onion, seasonings and cooked rice together, and place a quarter of the mixture like a sausage along the length of each pastry oblong. Brush egg wash over one long side. Fold the other part of the pastry over the sausage and crimp the edges together with a fork so that you have 4 long sausages.

With a pair of small scissors snip, snip along the middle to make the air vents, and then cut the strips of chicken roll into 2in (5cm) lengths (you should get about 10 per roll) and remove to a baking tray lined with some good greaseproof paper. Leave to chill in the fridge.

When you want to cook them, pre-heat oven to 450°F (230°C), Gas 8. Remove rolls from fridge and paint all over with egg wash. Place tray in oven, turn down to 425°F (220°C), Gas 7, and cook for about 20 minutes.

Stuffed Tongue Rolls

Serves 8
3-4 Granny Smith apples
½ pt (300 ml) home-made (or good bought) mayonnaise
2 oz (50 g) walnuts, roughly chopped
8 slices canned or fresh cooked tongue, about 2 oz (50 g) each

I have always been a lover of tongue (possibly because at times I have a very sharp one myself): I relish it in wafer-thin brown bread sandwiches with fresh mustard; I adore it cooked and served with a spiced cherry sauce; I covet very thick slices, dipped in egg and coated with breadcrumbs, fried and served with bought bottled sauce. Best of all I like it done this way and I was over the moon when I discovered that so many young people shared my view!

Wipe the apples clean, coarsely grate into the mayonnaise, and fold in the chopped walnuts. Lay the slices of tongue flat on your work surface and spoon the filling lengthwise about two-thirds across. Roll the slices of tongue up to resemble thick cigars. Transfer to a serving platter and sprinkle with chopped parsley. At times, for more sophisticated palates, I coat the tongue first very thinly with some mustard sweetened with soft brown sugar.

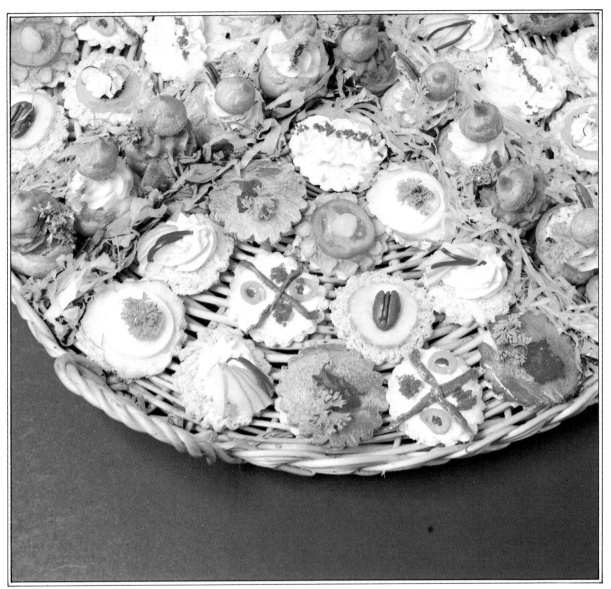

Previous page. *Create a garden room setting for a summer dinner party by massing house plants together. The central table arrangement, of roses and 'Bonnie Jean' spray chrysanthemums, features two impressive candle galleries. Start the meal with a cool and delicious savoury ham peach.*

Small round open sandwiches with a variety of toppings and garnishes are ideal for a summer garden party buffet, as are choux balls with tomato and avocado fillings. Arrange them decoratively on basketry or wicker platters to echo the summer basketry theme.

Chicken drumsticks marinated in yoghurt, ham on cheese scones, and deep-fried fillet of chicken breast with sesame seeds are ideal finger food for a summer garden party.

Bring a summer dinner party to a magnificent conclusion with that most famed of British puddings —summer pudding.

Create a train out of the simplest materials – an empty cola tin, cardboard boxes and tubes, and wrapping paper – as a cheerful table centrepiece for a children's party. This one is for Christmas, obviously, but the idea can be adapted for any time of the year. The little baskets filled with sweets make ideal – and inexpensive – going-home presents.

Below. Finish off a hearty children's tea with a green jelly field and a group of pear mice with pink eyes and vanilla pod whiskers and tails.

Serve orange cheese balls, triple decker fluted sandwiches, apple drop scones with home-made jam, and raspberry tartlets . . . and don't forget the mound of strawberries and cream.

Opposite. The magnificently romantic setting for the tea party is the lower lawn of the Miller Howe garden. Use the best china or silver, echo the colours of your plates and cups with napkins and home-made napkin rings, and decorate the table with a pretty and simple flower arrangement — here the container is an old condiment holder, which carries the jams and butters in the rings at the foot.

Emphasize your colour theme for a 4th July, Independence Day, picnic with accessories – the Stars and Stripes perhaps, a blue and white tablecloth, and red flowers. Serve the ham, roasted with beer and treacle, cold with spiced peaches.

Face Sponge Cake

These quantities will make 2 sponge cakes in 2 × 8in (20cm) round tins of about ³⁄₄in (2cm) deep.

Put the good soft butter and the sugar into a large warm bowl and combine by hand first before whisking and beating until the mixture is practically white in colour and very light in texture. Add the required weight of eggs, lightly beaten first, little by little. Mix each addition well in so that it is absorbed before adding more.

When the butter and sugar has taken in all the egg, fold in the flour carefully. Use a large metal spoon so that you don't knock out all that air you've beaten in. Pour into buttered, floured and sugared tins. Bake for 20-30 minutes in a pre-heated oven at 350°F (180°C), Gas 4. Take out of the oven, and leave for 15 minutes before turning out onto a wire cooling tray.

When cold, spread the top of one sponge generously with strawberry jam first, and then whipped sweetened double cream. Place the other sponge on top.

I'm not a dab hand at icing, so I kid myself that I don't want my end product to look 'professional' (it never would, I assure you!). Put the sieved icing sugar into a bowl, adding a touch of cochineal to give the face a pink colour, if you like, and add boiling water from the kettle little by little beating vigorously in between each addition until you achieve a thick batter consistency. Pour this over the cake and hurriedly with a small palette knife smooth it all over and down the sides. As it is setting sprinkle coarsely grated milk chocolate over the top half moon of the cake to look like hair (it looks quite punky and fashionable) and decorate the rest of the face with whatever you please.

4 oz (100-125 g) soft butter
4 oz (100-125 g) caster sugar
4 oz (100-125 g) eggs (weighed out of their shells)
4 oz (100-125 g) self-raising flour, sieved

Filling and icing
strawberry jam
double cream
12 oz (350 g) icing sugar
milk chocolate, grated
sweets for face features

Green Jelly Field Mice

Serves 4

2 fresh pears or 4 tinned pear
   halves
1 vanilla pod
8 pink peppercorns or silver cake
   balls
4 chocolate chips
5 oz (142 g) packet lime jelly

Fresh ripe pears should undoubtedly be used for this dish, as they are so much better. But if you decide to cheat and use tinned pear halves, I won't know...

If using fresh, then peel the pear with a stainless steel knife and cut in half through the stalk. Remove the core with a teaspoon, and make sure the thin stalk is removed too.

However expensive, I use fresh vanilla pods to make the spidery whiskers and straight pointed tail. (Tell the kids they can't eat them and then religiously collect them afterwards, wash and use for cooking!) Split the vanilla pods into thin lengths to make the ears and tail. Use pink peppercorns (available in delicatessens) or those lovely silver cake balls for the horrifically realistic eyes. Use a chocolate chip for the nose.

In slightly concave plates make green fields with packets of green jelly (use less water than the packet says to make sure it sets quite hard), and plonk the mice on top. Make individual green fields with a mouse for each guest, or larger fields with a meeting of mice.

Ice Cream Clowns

When asked to do these I immediately thought about home-made ice creams, which is so much richer and nicer – and then realized that kids these days are brought up on the bought stuff... for which I settled. The 'clowns' are scoops of ice cream on a tray (preferably metal), with faces on the ice cream and an ice cream cone or cornet clown hat on top. It's such a simple idea, and kids love it.

The most important thing is to have your serving tray very cold; leave it in the freezer for some time before the party. Or, if you have room, you could save some time by placing scoops of ice cream on the tray in the freezer. Then you need to work swiftly when actually serving and decorating the ice cream.

You need a packet – or packets – of cones, obviously, and, if you can be bothered, cartons of different flavoured and coloured ice cream. Use Smarties, chocolate buttons or any appropriate sweet for the eyes and nose. Make the mouth from a half piece of sugared fruit lemon or orange, or orange skin cut into quarter-moon pieces.

Children's Party

When it comes to organizing a party for children, something simple but special must be invented. Many people think that it's a waste of time going to too much trouble, that the children won't appreciate it – but how wrong some people can be. I organized my daughter's parties for years when she was at Infant and Junior school, and I think I might have had more fun than the children. Fortunately, she was born in high summer, so most parties were held outside, but an indoor party, although more messy, can allow your imagination to overflow with ideas – with themes, decorations, etc. It's all worth it when a jelly-covered lad comes up at the end and says, 'I had a smashing time, can I come next year?'

I always choose a particular colour scheme, with vibrant not subtle tones: bright reds and greens, green and yellow, or orange and pink. Look at the wonderful selection of paper ware that is available (think of the non-washing up afterwards) and choose your colours and any further ideas accordingly.

For a summer party in the garden, I would use a red gingham cloth to cover a trestle table, with red paper cups and napkins and a red 'cherry' tree. Fix a large jam jar to the trestle table leg with water in it to keep a branch of silver birch fresh. Try to get cherries in pairs, but if you can't persuade your greengrocer to pick through his selection of cherries, you can wire them together. Hang them over the branches to transform a birch into a cherry tree; the highlight of the party, just before they go home, is to raid the tree.

You could adapt this idea in any way you choose; if you're having a pirate party, hang foil-covered chocolate coins from your tree branch – or you could wrap up your (little) going-home presents and suspend them from the branch, or indeed from any handy tree in the garden. Or you could make your own tree (see page 156).

Another idea for a children's party is a train – made from the simplest materials – which could be the centrepiece of the table, and could be adapted for use at any party throughout the year. See the photograph between pages 80 and 81 for the end result.

I used small cardboard boxes, an empty cola tin, glossy wrapping paper, cardboard tubing, some ribbon and braid and cotton-wool. The small and medium cardboard boxes formed the open carriages and the base of the engine, covered in bronze and red shiny paper, which was folded neatly at the corners and sticky-taped on the underside. Strips of thin gold ribbon then went around the top, glued at the corners and at the start, and finish. A box was cut down in size to make the engine cab and measured to the size of Santa. This was also covered in wrapping paper and glued into position.

The main body part of the engine is the cola tin covered firstly at the end so that all the folded edge could be caught in the flat sheet of paper wrapped round the body (some braid was glued around this joining edge to keep it tidy looking). Now glue the body onto its base. The chimney was made from a piece of cardboard tubing covered in paper, edged in braid again, and glued into position. The buffers on the engine are 2 round Liquorice Allsorts glued on; the smoke is a piece of stub wire with cotton-wool threaded onto it; and the last things, the wheels – Jammy Dodger biscuits – were glued into position (and dc let them set well before standing upright as they may collapse).

You can put whatever you like in the open carriages. I went for sweets and chocolate foil-covered coins, but small sandwiches, cakes or savouries will also do – it's up to you! A small gift of a red lacquered basket full of Liquorice Allsorts and decorated with a bow is left on each plate, not to be eaten but to be taken home (better than that piece of cake wrapped in a paper napkin, which looks like nothing on earth when it gets there!).

Tea Party on the Lawn
Serves 4-6

Orange Cheese Balls

Triple Decker Fluted Rounds

Strawberries and Cream

Apple Drop Scones with Home-made Jam

Raspberry Tartlets

Moroccan Mint Tea

On the day we took the photographs, the sun positively beamed, and the Miller Howe garden looked at its best! These past summers one has hardly been able to mow the lawn let alone have tea parties on it, and long hot summers seem to be a thing of the past. . . . But there's absolutely no reason at all why you can't have your summer tea indoors while you look out at the pouring rain and overcast clouds. One has to be realistic, and hopefully the unusual recipes will make up for it!

Orange Cheese Balls

Makes about 12-16 balls
8 oz (225 g) good full cream cheese
juice and finely grated rind of
* 1 orange*
about 6 oz (175 g) flaked almonds

Mix the cheese with the orange juice and rind. Chop the almonds, and toast in the oven until nice and brown. Take large marble-sized pieces of the cheese mixture, roll them in your palms to a nice round shape, and then roll in the browned almonds.

Place the coated balls on a tray and put in the fridge. You can also dust them with a touch of paprika or curry powder, and a hint of chopped parsley also provides a colour and taste contrast.

Triple Decker Fluted Rounds

Make these in exactly the same way as the open sandwiches made for the garden party (page 66). But this time, 1 slice, which gives 3 × 2in (5cm) fluted rounds, will produce 1 complete triple-decker sandwich.

*   Use and mix brown and white bread, as in the photograph (between pages 80 and 81), and seek out complete contrasts in fillings. Choose from any of the following:*

chutney
mashed avocado
pear strips with fennel tops
round thin slices of red apple
chopped smoked oysters
finely grated Cheddar with onion
*   juice*
duck liver pâté

mashed sardines
minced smoked salmon
chicken purée (see page 64)
mashed banana
shredded dressed spinach
finely grated carrot and ginger
peanut butter
raspberry and apple purée

cream cheese with lemon, a
*   cooked prune, capers or chopped*
*   watercress*
mashed cooked salmon
skinned, sliced, lightly sugared
*   tomato*
thin slices of cucumber marinated
*   in vinegar*

You can garnish them as we have done with these little piped twirls of cream cheese tarted up with very thin slices of radish, with matchstick lengths of celery, with parsley or thin slices of stuffed olive. Or you could buy those tiny heart/spade/diamond/club cutters (do beware, some aren't at all strong), and cut shapes out of red and green peppers.

Strawberries and Cream

Hull your strawberries correctly, removing the entire stalk and central core without breaking the flesh. I seldom wash my strawberries but, just at the last minute, I give them a coarse sprinkling of freshly ground black pepper and then a coating of vanilla sugar. You can serve them with any kind of cream, but I personally prefer to serve a lightly whipped double cream flavoured with the merest taste of brandy and vanilla sugar.

Apple Drop Scones

Mix all the dry ingredients together and then gently rub in 1 oz (25 g) of the soft butter. Beat the eggs, milk and lemon juice together, make a well in the flour and add the liquid, stirring the flour in slowly until you have a smooth paste mixture. Grate the apple very finely directly into the paste.

Heat your griddle pan, paint liberally with the remaining butter, and place 3 dessertspoons of the mixture on the griddle at a time. When the base is cooked, turn over with a palette knife or spatula. As they are cooked, store in a folded tea towel on a plate to keep warm.

Serve with butter and some delicious home-made jam.

Makes 15-18 scones
8 oz (225 g) self-raising flour
1/2 tsp salt
4 oz (100-125 g) caster sugar
generous pinch ground cinnamon
1 1/2 oz (40 g) soft butter
2 eggs
10 tbsp milk
12 drops fresh lemon juice
1 apple, peeled and cored

Home-Made Jams

Jam making is as much part of my summer life as Father Christmas is Christmas to kids. No matter whether I am making huge amounts for use at the hotel, or the odd jar for home, I must stock up my store cupboard during summer to see me through the autumn, winter and spring.

Anybody, but anybody can make jam and unless one is a fanatic, no special equipment is necessary. Patience and common sense are the main ingredients.

The Basic Steps
1. A wide saucepan is best and to make sure it is spotlessly clean I usually sprinkle the base and sides with salt and then use a cut lemon as a scrubber to shine the surface of the pan. Rinse with warm water and then wipe dry.
2. The fruit should always be quite dry and perfectly fresh, preferably slightly under-ripe. Weigh it carefully and add the juice of 1 lemon per 1 lb (450 g) of sugar recommended for use in the recipe. It is the presence of pectin, a natural setting agent, in all fruit that will help set the jam when cooked and gone cold, and this varies in all fruit (in fact, it varies from summer to summer, too). The lemon juice makes up for a lack of natural pectin and fruit acid.
3. Whenever possible, do please use preserving sugar or else granulated or lump, but try not to use fine caster, as this tends to sink to the bottom of your mixture. And never, but never, use soft brown or demerara, as they give the jam a burnt flavour.
4. Put fruit into thoroughly clean saucepan, just cover with cold water, and simmer over medium heat until fruit drops and is quite soft. Always have the sugar nice and warm before you start

adding it to the slightly puréed fruit. When the sugar is all dissolved (you will have to stir constantly during this part of the jam making), bring to the boil and boil rapidly. When it looks as if it is ready, start the testing if you haven't a thermometer (the correct temperature is 220°F or 104°C).

5. You shouldn't require a sugar thermometer, as it is easy enough to know when the jam is ready for bottling by simply placing a teaspoon of the bubbling mixture onto a perfectly clean, cold saucer. Pop it into the fridge to let it cool quickly, then bring it out, and push it gently from the edge to the middle with your finger. If it wrinkles on each side and leaves a gap, the jam is ready. If it doesn't wrinkle, and the jam runs back after your finger has been pushed through, the jam isn't ready – carry on boiling.

6. Meanwhile all your jars and containers should have been washed sparkling clean in hot, soapy water, rinsed, and well dried with a clean towel. Keep them warm in the warming drawer of your oven, or in the oven itself. Fill the warm pots when the jam is ready and has been skimmed, while it is still hot.

7. Place commercial waxed discs on top of the hot jam (waxed side next to jam!) and then immediately cover each jar with a clingfilm or cellophane top, dampened on the outside. Press the covering edges down around the top lid of the jar, secure with rubber band, and then stretch. Leave to one side until cool and then store in a dark cool place.

Fresh Apricot Jam

2 lb (900 g) fresh ripe apricots
juice of 2 lemons
2 lb (900 g) preserving sugar

Halve the apricots and place in pan, with stones, and simmer in lemon juice and water until pulpy before adding sugar. When dissolved, bring to the boil. Pick out the stones before bottling.

Dried Apricot Jam

1 lb (450 g) dried apricots
3 pt (1.7 l) cold water
juice of 3 lemons
3 lb (1.4 kg) preserving sugar

Soak the apricots for 24 hours in the water (stirring and turning occasionally), add the lemon juice and simmer for 30 minutes before adding the sugar.

Rhubarb Jam

2 lb (900 g) prepared rhubarb (see method)
juice of 2 lemons
2 lb (900 g) preserving sugar

Top and tail the rhubarb, skin it, and cut each stick into 2in (5cm) lengths. Weigh it to get the precise 2 lb (900 g). Instead of cooking straightaway, leave ingredients mixed together overnight, and then make the jam in the usual way. Don't add any water.

Two delightful changes can be made to this relatively cheap jam. Use as much or as little preserved or root ginger as you like in the boiling (if using root, do remember to peel it, cut into large pieces, with a wooden cocktail stick through each to remove easily); or, for a genuinely superb jam, add 4 generous handfuls of scented red rose petals to the jam as you start to bring it to the boil.

Blackcurrant Jam

Simmer until soft before adding sugar.

2 lb (900 g) blackcurrants, without stalks
juice of 2 lemons
2 lb (900 g) preserving sugar

Raspberry Tartlets

Make the pastry as described on page 54, and roll out. Cut to fit whatever type of tartlet tin you fancy – but I think the boat shape and fluted round are best for these. This quantity of pastry will make approximately 8-10 × 3in. (7.5cm) shapes. Bake them and cool them and then fill.

This cream cheese filling isn't quite as sweet as pure sweetened cream. Whip up the cream cheese with the double cream, add caster sugar, then fold in the beaten egg white. Spoon onto the base of the tartlets. Arrange the raspberries on top of the cream filling, and just before serving sprinkle with a little vanilla sugar, Some people make a redcurrant jelly glaze, but that isn't for me, as I just like to taste the fruit.

Pastry
1/2 lb (225 g) plain flour, less 2 tablespoons
tiny pinch of salt
3 tbsp icing sugar
5 oz (150 g) softened butter
1 egg, at room temperature

Filling
4 oz (100-125 g) soft cream cheese
1/4 pt (150 ml) double cream
1 tbsp caster sugar
1 egg white, beaten stiff
1 or 2 punnets fresh whole raspberries

Moroccan Mint Tea

A really hot day means I can serve my favourite of teas – Moroccan Mint. I have an unusual way of preparing it, and most people love it.

In a very warm 1 1/2 pint (900 ml) china teapot put the tea, teabags and fresh mint leaves (remember that when you ice it, it is 'let down'). Pour boiling water over the leaves and bags. Leave for 15 minutes and then pour through a tea strainer into whatever container you plan to use, and when cold put in the fridge.

I usually serve my mint tea in cut glass whisky tumblers, garnished with individual sprigs of fresh mint along with 2 or 3 freshly picked rose petals (I've never been conventional) and 2 lumps of ice. It is so thirst-quenching and refreshing.

Serves 4-6
2 teabags of personal choice
3 heaped tsp Earl Grey tea
15 (at least) fresh mint leaves
fresh mint sprigs
rose petals
ice cubes

Tea Party on the Lawn

Nephrolepis ferns
Senecio (*greyi*)
Pinks ('Doris')
Roses ('Carol')
Summer heathers
Hebe
Ribbon bows

Romantic that I am, I would love to see the return of the gracious days of the tea party, of a little elegance. In all those turn-of-the-century books I cannot recall them ever having a wet day when they wanted to have tea on the lawn; it was always fine and warm. So, choose your day carefully, and go all the way with your food, trimmings, and decorations — we're romantics, remember!

The delicate colouring of my Victorian tea service (see the photograph between pages 80 and 81) gave me the theme and colour scheme for this particular tea party. Swathes of pink roses, forget-me-nots and blue entwined ribbon bows garland the china, so I wanted to keep this theme going through the tea party setting. Pick up the pink with a pale pink linen tablecloth, say, and have linen napkins in the blue of the china ribbon bows, simply rolled and slipped into home-made napkin rings (see page 42 for details on how to make them). The flowers, too, with added small blue ribbon bows, also carry on the chosen colour scheme.

As for the container, I found an old condiment holder in a local junk shop, and with 4 silver coasters sitting in the empty circular spaces, it was ideal for butters and jams (I have also used it on a dinner table for after-dinner mints). I managed to find a small dish to just fit the top metal ring, into which I taped the soaked floral foam for the arrangement.

An arrangement such as this will be viewed from all sides, so once the container is positioned, work from all sides, not just the front. Start off with the placement of 5 pieces of outline foliage flowing gently to the sides and with a central straight piece to create the height. Following the same lines, place your flowers — always the smaller ones first — and come to the large flowers towards the centre. Always remember that the larger or darker flowers should be a focal point towards the centre.

The flowers are 'Doris' pinks, 'Carol' roses, summer heathers and hydrangea heads; the foliages are nephrolepis ferns, senecio (greyi) and hebe. Blue ribbon bows tucked into the arrangement complete the romance (see page 145 for details on how to tie the perfect bow).

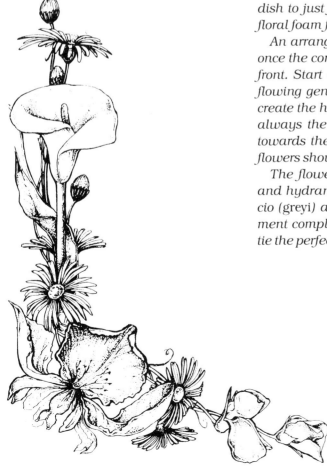

Independence Day Picnic
Serves 6-8

Tomato and Spinach Tart

Chilled Curried Courgette Soup *or* Cranberry and Orange Soup

Boiled Chicken

Walnut Oil Dressing

Roast Ham with Beer and Treacle, with Sweet Mustard Sauce
and Spiced Peaches

Lakeland Meat Loaf Slice

Fruit in Melon Cases

Blueberry Cream Pie
or
Blueberry Buns

On 4 July 1776 the 13 colonies of North America became independent of Great Britain. The day is a national holiday in the United States, and as it's high summer, it's usually celebrated by a cook-out or barbecue, or a picnic – at both of which the Americans excel. Never being one to miss out on a party occasion, I thought we'd join in!

That American delicacy, the blueberry, is now available in Britain (grown in Dorset), and the pie and buns make full delicious use of their flavour.

Tomato and Spinach Tart

Serves 8

*1 baked 10in (25cm) flan case
    (see page 54)*
4 tomatoes
*1 lb (450 g) frozen spinach
    (defrosted weight)*
2 oz (50 g) butter
6 oz (175 g) cream cheese
3 eggs, beaten
*2 oz (50 g) Parmesan cheese,
    grated*
*1/4 pt (150 ml) double cream,
    lightly beaten*
2 oz (50 g) pine kernels, toasted

Skin tomatoes, cut in half through their equator, and remove seeds. Cook spinach as directed on packet, drain well, and dry out as much as possible before mincing it. Cream the butter with the cream cheese and minced spinach, then little by little add the eggs with the Parmesan cheese and the cream. Fold in the lightly toasted pine kernels (simply toast by spreading on an oven tray and cooking in a slow oven until nice and brown).

Place the 8 tomato halves flat side down in a circle close to the outside edge of the cooked flan case on a baking tray, then pour on the creamed spinach mixture. Bake in a pre-heated oven set at 375°F (190°C), Gas 5 for 45 minutes. Leave to cool on the tray, and carry to picnic still inside its (preferably loose-bottomed) tin to prevent damage.

Chilled Curried Courgette Soup

Serves 8

4 oz (100-125 g) butter
8 oz (225 g) onions, finely chopped
*2 lb (900 g) courgettes, thinly
    sliced*
1/4 pt (150 ml) dry sherry
1 tbsp curry powder
1 1/2 pt (900 ml) chicken stock

Melt the butter in a large saucepan, and sauté the onions. When soft, add the courgette slices, sherry and curry powder. Cover with a double thickness of well dampened greaseproof paper and simmer slowly for 45 minutes. Put into liquidizer goblet with the chicken stock and liquidize.

Pass through a fine sieve into a bowl and when cold put in the fridge to chill. Serve with a dessertspoon of coarsely grated courgette and a wedge or slice of fresh lime.

Cranberry and Orange Soup

Serves 8

4 oz (100-125 g) butter
8 oz (225 g) onions, finely chopped
2 lb (900 g) defrosted cranberries
6 tbsp redcurrant jelly
juice and rind of 3 oranges
1/2 pt (300 ml) natural yoghurt
1/2 pt (300 ml) single cream

Melt butter in saucepan and lightly fry the onions. Add cranberries, redcurrant jelly and orange juice and rind. Cover with a double thickness of dampened greaseproof paper, and simmer over a low heat for 45 minutes. Liquidize and pass through a sieve.

Fold in the yoghurt and cream when cold, and adjust the seasoning – it may require some sugar. Serve chilled, garnished with additional whole defrosted cranberries and orange segments.

Boiled Chicken

I discovered this method of cooking chicken when I was in Hong Kong. I spent most of my tourist visit literally sniffing my way around the streets and the delightful smells of food – particularly at the car park for the sailings to Macao, which in the evening becomes a huge outdoor restaurant where you eat wandering from stall to stall, picking, choosing, devouring, enjoying!

Remove giblets from chicken, and wipe the inside and outside. Choose a saucepan or casserole just big enough to hold the bird and then fill the pan with cold water to just cover the bird. Remove the chicken and put to one side. Add salt and finely chopped spring onions to the water, cover with a piece of foil and a lid, and bring to the boil.

Lower the chicken into the boiling water, immediately bring back to the boil, and cook swiftly for 10 minutes only. Leave the chicken in the pan with the water but *under no circumstances lift the lid off*. The chicken will be cooked to a turn when it is cold – which will be about 8 hours after cooking. Remove the chicken from the water, rinse in very cold water, and pat perfectly dry. Brush all over with the walnut oil and finally sprinkle with salt and pepper.

When ready to serve, cut and portion in the usual way, and serve a salad dressed with the following walnut oil dressing.

Serves 6-8
1 fresh farm chicken, about 3 lb
* (1.4 kg) in weight*
1 tsp salt
4 spring onions, chopped
3 tbsp walnut oil
salt and freshly ground black
* pepper*

Walnut Oil Dressing

A firm favourite of mine but now I make it less powerful (walnut oil is very heavy). It's easily made in a liquidizer.

Combine all the ingredients at a low speed if possible. Transfer to a container and chill. By the next day the heavy oil will have dropped to the bottom of the container – but leaving its heavenly taste behind – and you simply strain off the top part to use for your mixed or green salad.

3 tbsp wine vinegar
¼ pt (150 ml) walnut oil
¾ pt (425 ml) good olive oil
pinch of salt, and freshly ground
* black pepper*
1 tsp English mustard
2 tsp sesame seeds
¼ pt (150 ml) red, white or rosé
* wine*
1 tsp caster sugar
1 tsp runny honey

Roast Ham with Beer and Treacle

1 ham
black treacle
cloves
demerara sugar
vegetable peelings (see method)
light ale or lager

The most important thing about this recipe is that you must be sure of the exact weight of the ham before you start. The size I would normally use is from 6 to 8 lb (2.7-3.6 kg).

Put the ham into a large saucepan, cover completely with cold water and leave in a cool place for 48 hours. Each morning and evening pour off the water and replace with fresh; the ham will therefore have 4 complete changes of water before you start cooking it. Start to cook in fresh water yet again.

Allow 20 minutes per 1 lb (450 g) for the initial boiling along with 1 tablespoon black treacle per 1 lb (450 g): so a 6 lb (2.7 kg) ham will therefore simmer away for 2 hours after being brought up to boiling point, along with 6 tablespoons black treacle. Allow to cool before removing from the water: the ham will look pretty grotty at this stage – very dark and a little sticky.

With a sharp knife carefully cut away the skin and reveal the soft juicy fat. Make criss-cross incisions into the fat, making lots of diamond shapes and in the middle of each diamond firmly push a clove. Coat the whole surface generously with demerara sugar and then put the ham into a roasting tray lined with roughly chopped vegetable peelings – the onion skins, parsley stalks etc.

Then for each original 1 lb (450 g) of fresh ham you need ¼ pint (150 ml) light ale or lager – so for the original 6 lb (2.7 kg) ham, 1½ pints (900 ml) are required. Heat this in a separate saucepan, pour on to the base of the roasting tray, and then cook the ham in a pre-heated oven at 375°F (190°C), Gas 5 for 10 minutes per lb (450 g).

Serve cold for a picnic obviously – it's delicious – but it can be served hot, with the warm mustard sauce and spiced peaches.

Sweet Mustard Sauce

2 oz (50 g) butter
about 6 oz (175 g) onion, finely chopped
4 tsp Moutarde de Meaux
2 tbsp demerara sugar
1 tbsp sherry vinegar
1 tbsp plain flour, sieved
½ pt (300 ml) double cream

Melt butter in saucepan and fry onion until golden. Add the mustard, the sugar and vinegar and combine well. Sprinkle on the plain flour and cook over medium heat for 5 minutes, stirring to make sure it doesn't stick. Put into liquidizer and blend, then pass through plastic sieve.

In a medium saucepan heat the double cream gently, then stir in the sieved mustard mixture and simmer for 10 minutes.

Spiced Peaches

Stick 3 cloves into each whole fresh peach and poach gently in a stock syrup made up of the water and cube sugar. Don't poach for too long, as you want the peaches firm enough to cut in half.

Put the peach halves onto a baking tray, sprinkle liberally with wine vinegar, and very finely with some ginger and a little paprika. Put a knob of butter on each.

When you wish to serve them hot put under a hot grill for about 3 minutes to heat through. Serve hot with cold or hot ham, or they are quite delicious to take cold to accompany your picnic ham.

4 fresh peaches
12 cloves
½ pt (300 ml) water
1 lb (450 g) cube sugar
wine vinegar
ground ginger
paprika
butter

Lakeland Meat Loaf Slice

An economical dish that can be made, virtually, on the spur of the moment for a family lunch or picnic. It's an idea, too, to make two meat loaves by doubling the quantity and freezing one for emergency use another day.

Combine all the ingredients in a large bowl and then press them down into the greased loaf tin. Pre-heat oven to 375°F (190°C), Gas 5. Put the loaf tin into a roasting tray with about 1½in (3-4cm) boiling water coming up the sides, and bake for 45 minutes.

Remove from oven, cover and put weights on top or packets of sugar (anything to simply press the meat down). When cold, re-move from tin and slice. (Or wrap in clingfilm and then in a double thickness of foil and freeze.)

Fills a 1 lb (450 g) loaf tin
8 oz (225 g) belly pork, coarsely minced
4 oz (100-125 g) cooked ham, cubed
2 oz (50 g) red peppers, finely diced
1 tbsp green peppercorns
1 tbsp tomato paste
1 tbsp runny honey
2 tbsp double cream
1 tbsp chopped fresh chives
1 tbsp finely chopped parsley
pinch of salt

Fruit in Melon Cases

This is an ideal pudding to serve at a picnic, as long as you remember to take a sharp knife, because everything can be taken along separately and safely, and then put together with consummate and delicious ease once you're at the chosen spot.

Choose any type of melon, and allow one half melon per person. Simply cut the melons in half – you can then vandyke with V's all round if you like – and remove the seeds and stringy flesh. Fill the hole with fresh fruit – see page 58 for the vast choice you have at this time of year. I like to sprinkle the fruit just before serving with lots of ice-cold vodka. Garnish with mint leaves.

Per person
½ melon
at least ¼ lb (100-125 g) fresh soft fruit
vodka
mint leaves

Blueberry Cream Pie

Serves 8
1 × 10in (25cm) cooked flan case
   (see page 54)
½ oz (15 g) gelatine
3 tbsp blackcurrant cordial
2 tbsp water
2 eggs, separated
3 oz (75 g) caster sugar
½ pt (300 ml) double cream
4 oz (100-125 g) blueberries,
   cleaned

Sprinkle the gelatine on the base of a small saucepan, and add the blackcurrant cordial and water mixed together. Leave to one side.

Put the 2 eggs yolks in a small warm bowl and beat away, adding the caster sugar little by little. Lightly beat the double cream and combine with the egg yolk mixture. Fold the blueberries in gently.

Put the saucepan of gelatine and cordial over a very low heat until reconstituted, then pass through a fine sieve into the cream/yolk mixture, and combine well, but gently. Beat the 2 egg whites until stiff and fold in. Spread over the cooked pastry base and leave to chill.

You can make a Macadamia Nut Orange Cream Pie in the same way. Grate the rind off 2 oranges, then reduce the juice to 5 tablespoons in which to reconstitute the gelatine. Add the rind to the egg yolks, and line the base of the flan with the segments from 3 further oranges. Top the orange cream with 2 oz (50 g) chopped and toasted macadamia nuts.

Blueberry Buns

Makes about 18 small buns
8 oz (225 g) butter
6 oz (175 g) caster sugar
3 eggs, lightly beaten
2 oz (50 g) cornflour
6 oz (175 g) self-raising flour
5 oz (150 g) fresh blueberries (or
   canned, but drain them well)

Blueberries are quite delicious in farmhouse pies (to give an added touch combine them with finely grated orange rind and sprinkle with a touch of good dark rum). Blueberry muffins are often served for breakfast in the United States – wonderfully fattening. These are nice for breakfast too, served straight from the oven, but they taste equally delicious cold with butter.

Cream butter and sugar together until light and fluffy then gradually beat in the beaten eggs. Fold in the sieved cornflour and self-raising flour, followed gently by the whole blueberries.

Dollop into paper cases, which are standing in patty tins, and bake in a pre-heated oven at 350°F (180°C), Gas 4 for about 20-30 minutes. Sprinkle generously with icing sugar before serving.

Independence Day Picnic

To some people the idea of an outdoor flower arrangement might seem crazy — and particularly one for a picnic. Obviously if you're travelling miles in the car, and then trekking across country to reach your picnic place, you would understandably feel reluctant to lug along flowers and foliage as well as the food! But picnics can be held at the bottom of the garden too, and flowers just add the finishing touch to the occasion. And why not?

On a day like this, a great day for the United States (though Great Britain wasn't too pleased at the time), it's imperative to create and emphasize your theme. Red, white and blue are the colours of the Stars and Stripes (as for the Union Jack, ironically), and you could hire a flag if you liked, to hammer the point home. These colours are not the easiest to find in fresh plant material, but can be highly dramatic.

Use, therefore, lots of accessories to illustrate your theme — a blue and white tablecloth, blue, white or red napkins, flags, coloured plates, cutlery, etc. The flower arrangement, as simple or as sophisticated as you like, could be dominated by the red of your theme — with red carnations, red roses, and lots of bright green foliage. I think any picnic table would be enhanced by such beauty!

Have a nice day!

Autumn

Fruit

Apples · Blackberries · Cranberries · Damsons · Figs ·
Kumquats · Nuts · Pears · Plums

Vegetables

Beetroot · Brussels sprouts · Cabbage · Carrots · Celery ·
Horseradish · Leeks · Mushroom (field) · Parsnips · Pumpkin ·
Red cabbage · Swedes · Sweetcorn · Tomato ·
Turnips · Watercress

Game

Goose · Grouse · Hare · Partridge · Pheasant · Quail · Rabbit ·
Wild Duck

Herbs

Chervil · Chives · Dill · Marjoram · Mint · Rosemary · Sage

Autumn

Garden and Florist Flowers

Aster · Carnation (bloom and spray) · Chrysanthemum ·
Dahlia · Gaillardia · Gladiolus · Lily · Marigold · Pyrethrum ·
Rose · Rudbeckia · Zinnia

Foliage and Berries from the Garden

Autumn Colourings

Copper Beech · Tulip tree (liriodendron tulipifera*) · Mountain Ash*
(sorbus aucuparia*) · Smoke tree* (rhus cotinus) *· Virginia creeper*

Berries

Berberis · Cotoneaster · Mountain ash (sorbus aucuparia*) ·*
Ornamental Crab · Pyracantha · Rose Hips – rosa Moyesii
and rosa Rugosa *· Skimmia (japonica)*

Autumn Food

Autumn is always a bit of a relief for me, as I know that, as far as work is concerned, the worst is over and the end is in sight (I do enjoy my work, but it's tiring!). As the trees change colour I know that we can look forward to the tastes that are exclusive to autumn – the delicious English apples, plums and pears, the game, the best blackberries, and the first Brussels sprouts and parsnips (both so welcome after a season without). It's also the time when we in this country try desperately to make the most of the good weather before it finally disappears – and have barbecues with hot spiced cups and warming soups.

But the colder weather also signals the onset of stews and casseroles, and hot puddings, the pickling of the last of the summer fruits and vegetables, and the initial preparations for Christmas when the puddings are made and stored. Sadly, autumn also heralds the end of the fresh herb garden at the first hard frost – but I must admit that even after three light frosts the other year, our swamping borage still had its beautiful flowers, which we used to garnish starter plates.

Autumn primarily means to me the arrival of game. So many people rave on about the Glorious Twelfth (12 August) when the grouse season starts, but I wouldn't dream of cooking and eating grouse until at least mid-September, when the hanging has developed the flavour and texture of the flesh. Therefore three of the autumn menus feature game, and the other two give recipes suitable for barbecuing outside, should you be lucky enough to choose a warmish autumnal night!

Autumn Flowers

Season of mists and mellow fruitfulness. Foliage is changing colour everywhere and as the autumn advances there are all those colourful fruits, which you must beat the birds to; one day your mountain ash will look beautifully laden with berries, the next day it's bare!

As a flower arranger, the autumn is one of my favourite times because so much beauty can be gathered for free. Elderberry foliage, which turns such a subtle colour with its black fruits, is so useful; wild crab apples, snowberries and rose hips can also be included in arrangements; the berries of the hawthorn have wonderful long arching sprays and in late autumn shed all their leaves, leaving just the berries; bryony trails flow beautifully out of containers, as do the grey fluffy heads of Old Man's Beard.

It is not possible to preserve berries, but their life can be extended by a few weeks by spraying with varnish (that sold in art shops for spraying charcoal pictures). You can experiment too with glycerine treatment (see below). Leave the sprays of berries in the solution for about 2 weeks. Another useful thing to collect at this time of year is the bullrush or reed mace, which will shed its seeds all over the house unless you again spray with varnish. And don't forget cones and sprays of cones from firs, pines, cedars, spruces and larch.

Preserving

One of the easiest ways of preserving foliage for use at a later date is the glycerine method. Mix together one part of glycerine to two of warm water in a bucket and stir well. Use while the liquid is still warm, and the solution should come about 4in (10cm) up the stems (which should have been well prepared by splitting, etc, to let the fullest possible absorption take place). There are no set rules as to how long to leave the items in the liquid – everything depends on the variety of the leaf, the maturity of the branch, the temperature, and on whether you have measured the quantities properly. The colour changes gradually from its green through to pale cream to brown, and some things go almost black. Once the change of colour has taken place, take the branches out of the liquid.

It's vital to store your preserved materials properly. If possible, stretch a length of washing line across the attic or garage and suspend the branches from the line. Lay a sheet of polythene over the top to keep off the dust, leaving the air to circulate underneath.

Good leaves and branches for glycerine
Beech
Box (*buxus*)
Camellia
Choisya
Ivy (*hedera*)
Lady's Mantle (*alchemilla mollis*)
Laurel (*laurus*)
Oat
Solomon's Seal (*polygonatum x hybridum*)

Good flowers and leaves for drying

Acanthus

Achillea

Cardoon

Delphinium

Globe Artichoke

Grasses

Helichrysum (Everlasting or straw
  flower)

Love-lies-bleeding (*amaranthus
  caudatus*)

Sea Holly (*eringium maritimum*)

Pampas grass

Ferns

Allium

Pineapple plants and pineapples

Apples

Grapes

Plums

Bottles of wine

Rabbit

Game birds

Drying

You must harvest your flowers, seed heads and leaves, etc for drying at the right time – during dry settled weather after the dew has disappeared from the plants. They should be picked just as the flowers open or when the seed head begins to ripen and turn brown (full-blown flowers do not dry well). Simply hang small bunches of flowers, leaves and seed pods separately upside down in a dry and airy place (from that washing line again).

The large grouping of plant materials and accessories in the photograph between pages 120 and 121 is the sort of arrangement that I just love doing, and I think it looks like an Old Dutch Master painting. Most people haven't enough space for something like this, but don't forget it can be scaled down. A large old wooden chest in a hall or a table covered with some dark linen fabric would be ideal as a base for this sort of group, which will give you a little taste of what is to come in the following pages!

Against the oak panelling I placed the large wicker rice tray, giving some backing to the plant material. I needed three containers to take the arrangement, and each holds a piece of dri-foam. (I once met someone who was most upset because she'd waited all day for this new-fangled floral foam to take up water – she'd have had to wait a week or more!)

Start the arrangement by placing in the pampas grass, ferns and allium heads to give the height. Wicker fans, trays and further dried plant material were placed to get the width. The next stage was placing the old wine jars and bottles, which will be part of the focal point of the arrangement. I wanted also to give some fresh plant material interest, so I went for fruit and two decorative pineapple plants. The plants were taken from their pots with the soil, and put into plastic bags: a garden cane was then wired to the side of the plastic bag to act as a stake, and this was pushed into the dri-foam as if it were a flower stem. Pineapples, apples, grapes and plums were then placed in various areas naturally flowing amongst the dried leaves and seed heads. Bottles of wine, rabbits, and game birds complete the still-life.

As you can see, when using dried and preserved plant materials, it's the variety that creates interest. Always look for different shapes, colours and textures: matt surfaces against shiny, rough against smooth, and so on. Anyone fortunate enough to travel should never set foot outside the country without the flower arranger's plastic bag; it's such a pleasure to add to an arrangement something unusual, perhaps exotic, that has come from faraway places.

Formal Game Dinner

Serves 6

Vegetable Pistachio Cream on Tomato Provençale with Courgette
and Mustard Sauces

Roast Grouse with Bread Sauce, Oatmeal Potato Croquettes and
Fried Turned Vegetables

Pickled Kumquats

Brown Sugar Chestnut Meringues

This is a very special menu, and it needs a very special cook! Grouse are so delicious, the highlight of autumn as far as I'm concerned, and the accompaniments I recommend are tasty and different. The starter will madden and delight you, and the meringues will finish off your truly gourmet meal.

Do try and make the pickled kumquats — even if you normally never venture near a bottle of malt vinegar. Kumquats are available all year round, though in short supply, and the pickle is so easy. Although I recommend 21 days before sampling, the longer the better.

Vegetable Pistachio Cream on Tomato Provençale with Courgette and Mustard Sauces

Serves 6-8

8 oz (225 g) chicken breast
2 tbsp natural yoghurt
juice and grated rind of 1 fresh lime
4 tbsp pistachio nuts, shelled and skinned (see below)
2 eggs
¼ pt (150 ml) double cream
4 tbsp finely chopped raw vegetables (root preferably, but French beans, garden peas and red peppers can be used)
Tomato provençale (see below)

Courgette and Mustard Sauces

1 pt (600 ml) double cream
2 tsp Moutarde de Meaux
2 courgettes, boiled, puréed and sieved

After reading this recipe you will probably say 'Pistachio nuts to you too, Tovey, if you think I'm going to all that trouble!' I'm not off my head – but I must admit the recipe is a bit fiddly. You should have a bash, though, as this dish is always a winner, and worth every second spent on it. One of its many beauties is that all the work can be done the day before at least, and as it is quite rich and filling, a simple main course and pud can follow. In fact, if you were merely to serve cold ham and salad and a trifle afterwards, your guests would still leave your table feeling they'd had a feast!

Marinate the breast in yoghurt, lime juice and rind for 2 days, turning frequently. When ready to use, chop roughly. Skin the pistachios by putting them in a bowl and covering with boiling water straight from the kettle. Leave for several minutes and then fish out a few at a time. When rubbed between the thumb and first finger the skin will soon come off. Roughly chop.

Place the chopped chicken and marinade into the blender or processor and turn it on, adding the eggs one at a time, and then the double cream. Remove to a bowl and fold in the nuts and the raw chopped vegetables. Spoon into the buttered seasoned ramekins and place in fridge until needed.

Make the sauces the day before too. To make the courgette and mustard sauces, place the double cream in a large saucepan and simmer away over a low, low light until reduced by half. Divide this between two very small saucepans. Mix into one the mustard, and into the other the courgette purée. Warm through very gently in double saucepans while the creams are cooking in the oven.

When you want to cook the creams pre-heat oven to 400°F, (200°C), Gas 6, and put ramekins in a bain marie of boiling water. Place in oven and cook for approximately 30 minutes. They will puff up like miniature soufflés.

Coat the base of your individual serving plates with warmed tomato provençale. Turn the vegetable cream out into the middle of this and cover the top of each, half with the mustard sauce, half with the courgette sauce. Top off with a sprig of parsley and serve at once (and yes, you do deserve that extra glass of wine after all that).

Tomato Provençale

Melt 2 oz (50 g) butter in a saucepan, and fry 4 fat cloves of garlic crushed with 2 teaspoons salt, and 4 oz (100-125 g) finely chopped onions. Add 1½ lb (700 g) roughly chopped tomatoes and simmer slowly for at least 1 hour. Warm through gently while the creams are cooking, and if there's any left over, it freezes well.

2 oz (50 g) butter
4 cloves garlic
2 tsp salt
4 oz (100-125 g) finely chopped onions
1½ lb (700 g) roughly chopped tomatoes

Roast Grouse

My main grouse about grouse is that it isn't until they are actually out of the oven that you know how tough or tender they are! So I usually cook 3 for 2 people, 6 for 4, or 8 for 6. If they all do turn out quite well I am not averse to having the tender unused one(s) the next day cold for lunch.

It is absolutely essential that your poor little birds should have been hung from their necks for at least a week, and before they are plucked you should be able to pull the tail feathers out easily. I can never for the life of me see why restaurateurs get so excited each 12th of August and proudly announce to the world that they are serving the first grouse of the season – when no self-respecting gourmet would look at one before the 21st!

Serves 6
6-8 grouse
4 oz (100-125 g) butter per bird
4 juniper berries per bird
sea salt

High cooking for a short period is my version, but I am pretty generous with the butter I put inside the ribcage and rub all over the bird. The juniper flavour isn't to everyone's taste, and certainly it isn't essential. Melt the butter and put in blender with the juniper berries. Blend well, then return to a pan and heat. Brown the grouse all over in the flavoured butter then roast in a preheated oven set at 450°F (230°C), Gas 8 for 25 minutes.

Serve at once, not forgetting to pour the flavourful juices over the birds. You could also accompany them with game chips, bacon rolled round prunes, and cranberry sauce.

Bread Sauce

Bring the milk to the boil with the onion and sage leaves. Add the breadcrumbs and simmer gently for 10 minutes. Remove from the heat and discard the onion and sage leaves.

Beat in the cream, butter and onion salt, until nice and smooth. Taste at this stage: add more salt if necessary, or a little sugar if too salty. Leave in a double saucepan until required and then it takes about 20 minutes to heat through.

¾ pt (425 ml) cold milk
1 small onion, peeled and stuck with 6 cloves
2 sage leaves
2 oz (50 g) fine white breadcrumbs
1 tbsp double cream
1 oz (25 g) butter
pinch of onion salt

Oatmeal Potato Croquettes

*1 lb (450 g) potatoes, peeled and
   evenly chopped*
½ oz (15 g) butter
2 oz (50 g) onions, finely diced
*1 oz (25 g) walnuts, finely
   chopped*
*1 tbsp chopped fresh parsley or
   chives*
2 tbsp double cream
2 eggs
8 tbsp porridge oats
oil for deep frying

Cover potatoes with salted water (be fairly generous with the salt at this stage), bring to the boil, and simmer until barely tender. While they're boiling, heat the butter in a frying pan and fry the onions, walnuts and herbs.

Strain the potatoes and put back into saucepan over low heat to dry out. Mash them smooth, beating in the double cream and 1 of the lightly beaten eggs. Fold in the cooked onion mixture.

Divide mixture into 12 even portions (2 per guest) and roll out into a sausage shape. Put on a tray, cover, and chill in the fridge for at least a couple of hours (or overnight if you like).

Lightly beat the remaining egg with 1 tablespoon water and roll each sausage in the mixture before rolling in the porridge oats. Once again chill until firm.

Pre-heat deep fryer or pan of oil to 360°F (170°C) and fry for 10 minutes. Serve immediately.

Fried Turned Vegetables

Serves 6
*8 oz (225 g) each of carrots,
   parsnips and turnips, peeled*
olive oil
butter
sea salt
freshly ground black pepper

Cut root vegetables into chip-size pieces about 2in (5cm) long, and as thick as your thumb (the stockpot should benefit from this rather extravagant dish, or use in a soup). With a small sharp stainless-steel knife, 'turn' each 'chip' from middle to each end until it looks like a mini cucumber. Leave to soak in water while you finish the rest.

Fill a saucepan large enough to hold a metal sieve with salted water, and bring to the boil. When boiling, submerge the sieve holding the carrots in the water. Bring back to the boil and cook for 2 minutes (a sort of basic blanching). Do the same, separately, with the turnips and parsnips.

When you wish to finally cook and serve, coat a small frying pan with a smear of olive oil and when smoking add a similar amount of butter. Place the par-cooked, drained, dried vegetables in the pan and toss-fry for 4 minutes. Season liberally with sea salt and freshly ground black pepper and serve at once.

The vegetables taste even better if you fry a tablespoon of finely chopped onions and mix with the cooked vegetables. Sprinkle generously with chopped parsley.

Pickled Kumquats

Kumquats are the tiny orange-like fruit of a shrub originally from Japan, but they are now grown extensively in various parts of the world, in abundance in the eastern Transvaal of South Africa.

I love kumquats as they are, raw and ripe, but they are quite delicious when pickled, served with duck, game and home-made terrines.

1 lb (450 g) kumquats, wiped
   clean with damp cloth
1 pt (600 ml) malt vinegar
4 tbsp brown sugar
12 cloves
1 tbsp black peppercorns

Bring the vinegar, sugar, cloves and peppercorns to the boil in a saucepan and simmer for 10 minutes. Put the wiped kumquats in a glass bowl or jar, and pour the slightly cooled, strained vinegar mixture over them. When cold, top with greaseproof paper and seal. Keep for 21 days at least before serving.

Brown Sugar Chestnut Meringues

Meringues? No. Pavlovas? Perhaps. They're crisp on the outside and soft on the inside, and a welcome change on the meringue scene.

I always like to actually weigh out my egg whites, as the fresh free-range farm eggs I use do vary in size. Line your baking trays with the best quality greaseproof paper available.

8 oz (225 g) egg whites, nice and
   cold
8 oz (225 g) soft brown sugar
8 oz (225 g) caster sugar

Chestnut cream
12 oz (350 g) soft butter
12 oz (350 g) soft brown sugar
12 oz (350 g) unsweetened
   chestnut purée

Put the egg whites into your cold mixer bowl and beat at a high speed until firm and fluffy. Mix the sugars together, then little by little add to the egg whites. Meringues are meant to be light when cooked, and do remember that if you pour in too much sugar in one fell swoop the mixture will sink and never rise up light again.

When all the sugar is in and the mixture is quite stiff, take 2 large dessertspoons, and scoop a full measure of meringue out with 1 spoon and ease it off with the other spoon onto your lined trays. In all you should be able to make 24 meringues.

Bake for 1 hour in a pre-heated oven set at 300°F (150°C), Gas 2. After 1 hour, turn off oven and leave meringues there until oven goes cold, with the door slightly ajar.

To make the chestnut cream, beat the butter and sugar well together until light and fluffy, and then beat in the chestnut purée, ounce by ounce. Never use the sweetened purée for this dish, as it's too sweet, but if this cream is still too sweet for you, or too little in quantity, beat in ½ pt (300 ml) double cream to give a lighter textured filling. Sandwich meringues with the cream and top with a marron glacé, or half pecan or walnut.

Pineapples
Candles
Escallonia (*macrantha*)
Nephrolepis fern
Berberis (*thunbergii*)
Spray carnations and carnations
Lilium ('Enchantment')
Roses
Grapes

Formal Game Dinner

A formal dinner party calls for a formal arrangement, and I don't think you need silver candelabra to get the formal atmosphere. Candles, fruit and flowers can be combined to give just the right effect. The oval base comes into play again (see page 76), and keeps everything in order.

My favourite fruit, the pineapple, plays a big part in this arrangement. It's not only delicious to eat, but you can see from the photograph between pages 120 and 121 that it doubles as the candle holder! Firstly, cut any stalk away from the base so that the pineapple stands straight and firm. It may need also to stand in a shallow container, again to keep it firm and level. If the petal top of the fruit is a little full in the centre, pluck some of the petals out to create a more defined hole, as the candle must go a fair way down to stay firmly in place. You may also need some plasticine to wedge it. Place a shallow container holding the soaked floral foam in the centre of the base with a prepared pineapple on either side. You will then be able to see what space and shape your arrangement is going to be.

The outline of the arrangement is created by a lovely foliage with a sweeping line – Escallonia (macrantha). I like this foliage because it also produces a very delicate blossom and then star-shaped bracts appear when the blossom petals drop away. The other foliage is Nephrolepis fern. Start by placing a fern good and straight in the centre of the floral foam. Then side-lying pieces are placed in horizontal to the base, firstly the Escallonia and then the ferns. At this stage we know the height and width, and the space remaining that the flowers and foliage will fill. The next placements are pieces of the shrub Berberis (thunbergii) used shorter than the first placements, and which bring a deeper bronze colour into the arrangement. Once you are happy with the shape you are getting, take your first flowers – orange spray carnations – and follow the same line already created with the foliage. Do remember that you must work on both sides at once, with both flowing foliage and flowers, so that you get the all-round appearance. Lilium 'Enchantment' are the main flowers towards the centre, and 'Orange Sim' carnations lead towards the base, bringing the weight down to the base where it is needed. The final flowers are orange roses and a few buds from spray chrysanthemums in a very deep bronze red colour – again giving variation in colour and depth of colour.

So that the pineapples aren't too lonely, I have included some sweeping bunches of grapes. Remember never to put a full bunch of grapes into an arrangement; cut them into smaller clusters and reassemble them to look like a complete bunch. At least then a 'thief' will only take part of your arrangement!

108

Informal Game Dinner

Serves 6

Deep-fried Nut Cutlet with Tomato Provençale

Cabbage, Walnut and Bacon Salad with Garlic Croûtons

Boned Stuffed Quail with Grapes, and Fanned Roast Potatoes

Blackberry Sponges with Cassis Cream

I am fortunate in that I have a handy supply of boned quail, which, when bought, look like flattened frogs (unappealing, I must admit, and repellent to some people). But with a rich stuffing piped into the belly (my stuffing swells up when cooking) the bird looks like a lovely oval ball of deliciousness (served on a mushroom croûton if you like). Quail are fiddly to eat normally, but if you can get hold of the boned ones, they'll be a wow at any dinner party.

If the fresh blackberries are well and truly on their way out, then I suggest you use some French bottled blackcurrants for the pudding.

Deep-fried Nut Cutlet with Tomato Provençale

Serves 6

3 tbsp sultanas
3 tbsp sherry
3 oz (75 g) each of shelled walnuts, pecan nuts, hazelnuts and almonds
1½ oz (40 g) onion, finely chopped
6 tomatoes, peeled and roughly chopped
2 cloves garlic, crushed with ½ tsp salt
freshly ground black pepper
pinch of nutmeg
6 oz (175 g) porridge oats or medium oatmeal
oil for deep frying
tomato provençale (see page 105)

These are ideal as standby dishes for the freezer, and excellent for vegetarian guests.

Soak the sultanas in the sherry overnight.

Place all the remaining ingredients, except for the oats, oil and tomato provençale, in a food processor and blend. Remove to a bowl and fold in the swollen sultanas.

Divide into 6 portions, shape to a lamb-chop shape or roll into a croquette shape and coat with the porridge oats or oatmeal. Chill for a couple of hours before frying, or you could freeze them at this stage.

Deep fry at 300°F (150°C) for 4-5 minutes until golden brown, and serve immediately with tomato provençale.

Cabbage, Walnut and Bacon Salad with Garlic Croûtons

Serves 6

3 slices stale bread
2 oz (50 g) butter
2 cloves garlic, finely crushed with ½ tsp salt
6 oz (175 g) smoked bacon
1 small green spring cabbage, washed and drained
4 oz (100-125 g) walnuts, chopped

Remove crust from bread slices, and then cut the slices into small cubes. Melt the butter in a frying pan, stir in the crushed garlic and add the bread cubes. Fry until golden brown, stirring with a wooden spoon, and keep hot.

Meanwhile cut the rind off the bacon, and chop the rashers into very small pieces. Fry these in the same pan until very crisp and well done.

Remove centre stems from the cabbage leaves and then shred finely. Scatter on small individual plates, and when you wish to serve, spoon on the warm crisp bacon bits and pour over any fat. Add chopped walnuts and warm croûtons.

Boned Stuffed Quail with Grapes

With more and more game being farm raised it is easier to purchase quail throughout the year. Although, at times, farmed quail lack the earthy flavour of the natural bird, they are invariably soft and tender. This is a fiddly dish, but when your guests see those deliciously fat plump small birds on the plates, slice through them seeing for the first time the superb rich filling – and you can hear the gasps as they have their first taste – your hard work will have been well worthwhile.

Serves 6
6 boned quail
12 oz (350 g) chicken breast, boned and skinned
3 tbsp natural yoghurt
3 eggs
7½ fl. oz (225 ml) double cream
salt and freshly ground black pepper
butter

Cut chicken breast into pieces, put in a dish with the yoghurt, and marinate for 24 hours. Put the chicken into a food processor and whizz round for a few seconds, dropping in the eggs one by one. When well combined, take the bowl off the machine and put in the fridge for at least 8 hours (or longer, depending on when you wish to finish the quail). Put bowl back onto the machine and dribble the cream in, a little at a time, with salt and pepper to taste.

Simply spoon this floppy mixture into the bellies of the quail. You will find it easiest to put wooden cocktail sticks through its 'bottom' and stand it thus. Close with another 2 cocktail sticks to keep the filling in, and put on a baking tray.

When you wish to cook them, bake for 30 minutes in an oven pre-heated to 400°F (200°C), Gas 6. Pour about 1 tablespoon melted butter over each quail, and baste once or twice.

Serve with a simple cream sauce – 1 pt (600 ml) cream reduced gently to about half, with seasoning to taste – and serve garnished with pipped grapes. A good accompaniment at this time of year is buttered baby Brussels sprouts, cooked for a few minutes only so that they are still crisp.

Fanned Roast Potatoes

Serves 6
at least 12 medium potatoes
walnut oil
salt
freshly ground black pepper
fat for roasting (see method)

A pretty sight on any main course plate, and so easy to prepare.

Peel your potatoes and cut to approximately the same size; then roughly shape to the same shape. Take a small slice off the base of each so that the potatoes will stand firm and square in the roasting tin, and then, using a small sharp knife, make cuts into the potato, going from the top to two-thirds down, all along the length of the potato so that it resembles a cock's comb.

Paint each potato with walnut oil, inside the cut edges as well, sprinkle with salt and freshly ground black pepper, and roast in your usual way (for at least 1 hour). I like to use duck fat or beef dripping, and if you've never tried either of these, do so as soon as possible – you'll be amazed at the difference in taste. The potatoes fan out during the cooking and look good – they also taste delicious and crisp.

Blackberry Sponges with Cassis Cream

8 oz (225 g) soft butter
8 oz (225 g) caster sugar, sieved
4 large eggs, lightly beaten
8 oz (225 g) self-raising flour,
 sieved
Crème de Cassis
double cream
blackberries

Believe it or not, to get this straight-sided soufflé effect, I cook these sponges in ramekin dishes. The basic Victoria sponge recipe is used and this 8 oz (225 g) mixing will fill 12 × 3in (7.5cm) ramekins.

Beat the butter and sugar together until light and fluffy, and then little by little beat in the beaten eggs. Fold in the sieved self-raising flour, with 2 tablespoons Crème de Cassis, if you like (this addition isn't absolutely necessary, but it tastes good).

Divide between the 12 buttered ramekins and bake at 350°F (180°C), Gas 4 for 20-30 minutes. Fill after cooling with Cassis-flavoured whipped double cream, plain cream or cream mixed with liquidized, sieved blackberries. Liberally scatter the cream with fresh blackberries.

Informal Game Dinner

Most people think that a door decoration is something that can be done only for Christmas, but there's absolutely no reason why this should be so. Autumn is an ideal season in which to utilize all those wonderful nuts, fruits and berries that are available, which look superb in this sort of welcoming arrangement.

I was demonstrating at a flower-arranging club in Germany when I came across a straw advent ring and I recognized its decorative potential straightaway (see the photograph between pages 120 and 121). If you haven't anything similar, see the ideas for a Christmas welcome ring (page 140); you could use any round basket disc shape, or even a covered base (see page 76) with a hanger.

As with any arrangement it's the foliage outline that is the start. Treated ferns were the first placements followed by ovate leaves cut from the bark of the coconut palm, with a wired stem attached (see page 31 for how to do this). The advantage of these straw rings is that no mechanics as such are needed; the wired stems are pushed straight into the straw. The centre fruit and nut part is a lovely collection of wooden grapes, brought back from the United States, cones, cone shapes made in a similar way to corn dollies, and dried leaves. The large flat cream coloured leaves – called grape leaves – were gathered on a holiday in Florida (never go anywhere without that plastic bag). The ring when completed was suspended from brown ribbon. Take the ribbon up over the top of the door and drawing-pin into the top thickness, which saves any damage to the wooden face of the door.

This same ring also makes an ideal table centre-piece used in its traditional flat form, and 4 candle placements are its main feature. These need to be well attached, so use 3 cocktail sticks sticky-taped to the ends of the candles with half the stick protruding below the candle. This creates a tripod that pushes into the straw. Again, as above, fruits, cones and leaves are wired and grouped around the candles, not too near or it could be bonfire night before its time. Complete the arrangement with bows of ribbon (see page 145).

Straw ring
Ferns
Coconut palm leaves
Wooden grapes
Cones
Wicker cones
Grape leaves
Ribbon

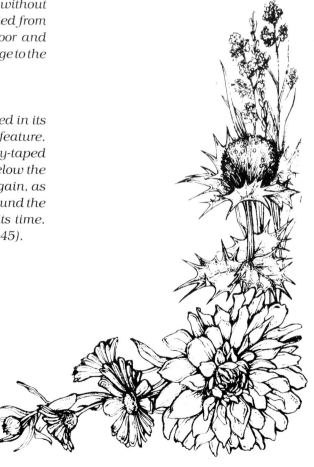

Hallowe'en Party

Serves 6-8

Pumpkin and Saffron Soup

Tomato Jam

Sausage Cartwheels with Turnip Fingers

Baked Potatoes with Port and Stilton Cheese

Poached Spiced Pears with Cinnamon

Treacle Toffee Apples

A Hallowe'en party can, of course, be indoors or outdoors, but is perhaps usually held in tandem with a firework bonfire party – the last occasions one can possibly entertain out of doors before winter proper sets in! The food is simple, delicious, and will keep your guests warm: you can cook everything in the oven, or on the barbecue, or you can cheat by doing a bit of both – starting the sausages and potatoes in the oven and finishing them over charcoal.

The remaining recipes – the soup, veg, jam, Stilton cheese, and pudding – can be prepared the day before.

Pumpkin and Saffron Soup

*Yes, I know real saffron is rather expensive, but it goes so
wonderfully with the pumpkin flesh you have carved out of your
lanterns, and if you are holding your party out of doors, it's very
warming. Serve it in mugs if you like.*

Serves 6-8
2½ fl. oz (75 ml) hot milk
2 good pinches of fresh saffron
4 oz (100-125 g) butter
8 oz (225 g) onions, finely chopped
2 lb (900 g) pumpkin, peeled and
  evenly chopped
¼ pt (150 ml) sherry
1 pt (600 ml) chicken stock

Pour the hot milk onto the fresh saffron and leave to infuse for
30 minutes.

Meanwhile melt the butter in a saucepan, add the onions, and
cook until nice and golden. Add the pumpkin and the sherry,
along with the infused saffron and milk. Cover with a double
thickness of dampened greaseproof paper and simmer for 30 minutes (the pumpkin falls quite quickly). Add the chicken stock.

Liquidize the soup (remembering never to fill the liquidizer more
than two-thirds full at a time), and pass through a sieve into a
clean container. When cold put in fridge or freezer (if you freeze it,
it loses a little of the saffron flavour and must, repeat must, be
reheated in a double saucepan). Otherwise take it straight from
the fridge to a saucepan and reheat gently over a low heat, about
25 minutes, and then taste. Adjust seasoning at this stage. Garnish just before serving with finely chopped parsley.

Tomato Jam

*I make this often, and it makes a delicious change from bottled
tomato sauce.*

2 lb (900 g) over-ripe tomatoes
rind and juice of 1 lemon
¾ lb (350 g) preserving sugar

Wipe the tomatoes clean with a damp cloth and quarter each one.
Place in a saucepan with the rind only of the lemon. Don't add any
liquid at this stage, but place over a low light and simmer away
gently for about 15-20 minutes until the tomatoes fall and become
mushy. Pass through a metal sieve into a bowl and stir in the
lemon juice.

Wipe out the saucepan and return the sieved tomato and lemon
juice to this and put once again over a low heat. Bit by bit stir in
the preserving sugar, and when all is combined, boil the mixture
for about 20 minutes. Test as for jam – a teaspoon of the mixture
should set when put on a cold plate. When cool, put into clean jars
and seal when cold.

Sausage Cartwheels

Serves 6-8

3-4 lb (1.4-1.8 kg) sausages
wooden cocktail sticks
sprigs of fresh herbs

In the English Lakes we are well blessed still with the traditional butchers who make their own sausages, particularly the world-famous Cumberland sausages. Visitors are always mesmerized by these festooned over marble slabs in the local butchers, and often take a yard or so away to remind them of the Lakes when they go home! At Miller Howe we cut small chunks off the yards delivered twice weekly and bake them in the oven as part of the Hearty Lakeland Platter served each morning for breakfast. I love them baked in the oven or barbecued, allowing a good ½ lb (225 g) per person.

Cumberland sausages can be obtained at places like Harrods, and elsewhere in the country a good local butcher who makes his own sausages would be only too pleased, I'm sure, to sell you X number of pounds not tied off in sausage lengths. Then you can easily make these delightful cartwheels.

Lay the length of sausage flat on your work surface and then slowly wrap to form a flat cartwheel shape, which you hold together with wooden cocktail sticks on 2 sides. And that's all you do!

If you intend roasting them in the oven, do so at 400°F (200°C), Gas 6 for 30-35 minutes, or they can be barbecued outside over charcoal. I like to garnish the sausages with sprigs of fresh marjoram, mint or parsley, and I always serve them with a good home-made chutney (see page 67), or the tomato jam above.

Posh people might want a knife and fork to eat them but I simply put the cooked hot cartwheel on a plate, remove the cocktail sticks, and break lumps off, dunking them in chutney before popping in my mouth (but then I'm a pig).

Turnip Fingers

Serves 6-8

2 lb (900 g) turnip
4 tbsp runny honey (at least)

Peel the turnips, cut into slices and then into lengths the size of large chips. Put into a pan of cold salted water, bring to the boil and cook for about 4 minutes. Remove from heat, strain and refresh under cold water. They will be quite crisp. They can be eaten cold with hot runny honey poured over or heated through in tinfoil as the sausages finish cooking. I personally prefer them cold with the runny honey.

Baked Potatoes with Port and Stilton Cheese

The port and Stilton cheese is ideal for baked potatoes when you're feeling extravagant, and a wonderful way of using the end bits of a Stilton. It's also a good standby to have in a jar in the fridge.

Allow 1 baking potato per person of between 8 and 10 oz (225-275 g), but if you have greedy friends like me, you should perhaps bake a few more, just in case. The only other thing you need is lots of sea salt. Wash and dry the potatoes well, and make a small cross-cut in the top of each. Imbed the potatoes in a layer of sea salt in a roasting tin, and bake for at least 2 hours in a pre-heated oven set at 425°F (220°C), Gas 7. Remove from the tray (you may need to use a little force), and push in and up to open the cut. Pipe or spoon in some of the port and Stilton cheese.

Port and Stilton Cheese

Simply bring together all the ingredients in a food processor and scrape into jam jars or other suitable containers. If it's not going to be used within a day or so, when chilled, seal with a little cool melted butter. Allow about 1 oz (25 g) per potato.

4 oz (100-125 g) old ripe Stilton
2 oz (50 g) soft butter
2 tbsp port

Poached Spiced Pears with Cinnamon

Use a saucepan that will take your pears nestling side by side so that they stand up securely.

Peel and core the pears, but don't remove the stalks. On the base of the pan put the cloves and the cinnamon, broken up into quarters. Place the peeled cored pears base down in the pan – they should be quite tightly packed – and press down through the stalks a double thickness of aluminium foil. Ease up a corner of this and pour in the red wine. Simmer for 1 hour over a very low heat.

When the pears are cooked, remove from the liquid and put to one side. Strain the liquid and measure what you have left – usually about ¾ pt (425 ml), and to each ¼ pt (150 ml) add 2 oz (50 g) soft brown sugar. Return to the heat and simmer until this mixture has reduced by half. As this syrup cools it becomes thick and dark red. Pour over the pears just before serving.

Serves 8
8 pears
8 cloves
2 sticks cinnamon
2 pt (a generous l) red wine
soft brown sugar

117

Treacle Toffee Apples

For 10 apples

1 oz (25 g) butter
12 oz (350 g) soft brown sugar
6 oz (175 g) runny black treacle
¼ pt (150 ml) water
1 tsp vinegar

Firstly, prepare your apples. Wipe and dry them thoroughly and push wooden skewers into the stalk end of each.

Weigh the butter first and on top of this weigh out the brown sugar and on top of this again the black treacle (this way there is no waste of treacle, which is a messy item to weigh anyway). Transfer all ingredients to a heavy saucepan (about 7in or 17.5cm in diameter).

Put over a gentle heat, and insert a sugar thermometer and a long-handled wooden spoon. Stir until the sugar is dissolved, then bring to the boil. After 2 minutes the volume will double and bubble up inside the pan, and after a further 6 minutes the temperature should just reach 290°F (143°C) – or when a drop in cold water snaps cleanly.

With a well buttered metal tray at your side, as well as the skewered apples, tilt the saucepan away from you, and dip each apple in the hot toffee in turn. Twirl the stick around and the toffee will collect on the apple. Transfer each apple to the greased tray, and leave to cool.

Hallowe'en Party

Carved pumpkin heads are traditional Hallowe'en decoration, and are so easy to make. If you can't get hold of pumpkins, turnips or swedes will do, but they're not so easy to carve, and are, of course, much smaller.

Carve off a lid about 6in (15cm) in diameter from the top of the pumpkin, and through this you can spoon out all the contents (which you then use in John's delicious soup). Try to keep the shell walls about 1in (2.5cm) thick, a bit thicker at the bottom, and carve carefully when reaching the edges: you don't want to go through. To ensure a good result for the features of the face, mark the pumpkin first with a thick felt pen: circles or oblongs for the eyes, a triangle for the nose, and a huge smiley shape for the mouth (it is a happy time of year). If you're feeling particularly artistic, you can mark in some gappy teeth for a good gruesome effect. Then cut out with a sharp kitchen knife. Scoop out a circle from the slightly thicker base of the pumpkin (an apple corer would do), which will hold the candle (making sure that the candle when lit is at least 2in or 5cm away from the lid when replaced). The larger the face features, the more light will welcome – and amuse – your guests as they arrive.

You could also have a flower arrangement to welcome your guests. The white-painted brickwork in the photograph between pages 120 and 121 is a magnificent foil for any arrangement, but a hanging arrangement like this, with a basket base, looks good anywhere. I use these basket cages suspended from the ceiling at different levels a lot, not just in the autumn. As you will have realized by now, I'm an aficionado of basketry!

Suspend the cages at different levels (I used lengths of binding cane which is subtle, and very useful for this type of suspension), and have the plant materials flowing to the left and right. The outline is made up of sprays of berries – mountain ash, glorious orange colours that you have to beat the birds to – and I have wired some large clusters together in the centre for the impact of weight and colour. I have kept the autumn colours with 'Orange Sim' carnations and small bronze chrysanthemums. Keep the left/right flow started with the foliage and berries, and do remember to recess the odd bloom into the centre of the cage.

I wired a small container onto the bottom of the cage – the weave was large enough for me to get my hands through – and taped in some soaked floral foam into which to place the arrangement. If you haven't got such baskets – but they're widely available now, and not too expensive – you could use a metal hanging basket, or improvise with a round metal lampshade frame.

Mountain ash berries
Carnations
Chrysanthemums

Firework Barbecue

Serves 6 upwards

Hot Spiced Fruit Cup

Kebabs

Lamb Steaks

Chips in Newspaper

Mushy Marrowfat Peas

Rum Sultanas, Raisins and Currants in Puff Pastry

I love fireworks, bonfires, simple foods, eating outside – actually I just love parties and food of all kinds!

I haven't gone into too much detail about kebabs, as everyone has their own favourite combination of meat or fish and vegetables – and timing so depends on the state of the barbecue coals. The lamb steaks, though, are wonderful, especially when pan-fried.

The combination of chips and mushy marrowfat peas is a real part of my northern childhood (a Scottish friend said chips with deep-fried small black puddings or haggis was her strongest memory), so I hope you enjoy the simple, but oh so satisfying tastes.

A magnificent arrangement of plant materials and accessories for autumn, this idea can, of course, be scaled down if space is at a premium. Use wickerwork, basketry, and all sorts of dried and preserved, as well as fresh, plant material, along with fruit, bottles of wine, and game – if you're not eating it!

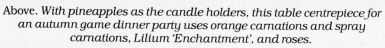
Above. *With pineapples as the candle holders, this table centrepiece for an autumn game dinner party uses orange carnations and spray carnations, Lilium 'Enchantment', and roses.*

Left. *End the dinner with nutty brown sugar chestnut meringues.*

Above. *Welcome your guests to an autumn game dinner party with a
door ring decorated with a grouping of dried and wooden material.
This same straw advent ring can also be used as a centrepiece of a
dinner table with candles as the main feature.*

Right. *Accompany the boned stuffed quail with baby Brussels sprouts,
fanned roast potatoes and a simple cream sauce, and garnish with
pipped grapes.*

Use the pumpkin flesh from the carved heads in a warming soup, to be followed by sausage cartwheels and baked potatoes.

Opposite. Welcome your guests to a hallowe'en party with a hanging basket flower arrangement, using the wonderful autumn berries and colours.

With the simplest possible materials – here an interestingly shaped branch, dried leaves and ferns, and globe thistle heads, all sprayed black – you can create a striking welcome arrangement for a firework barbecue. The scarlet 'sparklers' are made from humble drinking straws!

To capture the spirit of Thanksgiving or Harvest Festival, design an arrangement like this, using the wonderful colours, shapes and textures of fresh fruit and vegetables. Mount them all first on wooden rather than metal skewers, so that they will still be eatable after use.

Prepare your Christmas puddings in October before you become overwhelmed with all the other Christmas hustle and bustle. They taste all the better for the maturing, and should be stored in a dry, well-ventilated place.

Hot Spiced Fruit Cup

Soak the apricots overnight in the brandy.

Pour the wine into a large saucepan and add the sugar along with the strips of lemon and orange peel, nutmeg, cloves and cinnamon. Simmer for 10 minutes.

Warm ½ pt (300 ml) beer mugs and generously garnish with the assorted fruits, including the plumped-up apricots. Pass the hot wine through a fine plastic sieve into a jug and serve in the warmed fruit-filled mugs. Let the guests use their fingers to dig out the fruits; they will soon be warm inside and glowing outside and in the mood for a super party.

Makes 12 × ½ pt (300 ml) servings
12 dried apricots
¼ pt (150 ml) cooking brandy
2 bottles of light red wine
1 lb (450 g) caster sugar
scored peel from 1 lemon and 1 orange
1 whole nutmeg, finely grated
6 cloves
2 sticks cinnamon, broken into 2in (5cm) pieces

Garnishes
melon balls, pear slices, apple slices, orange wedges, seeded grapes

Kebabs

Small pieces of meat, fish or fowl threaded onto metal skewers along with vegetables are ideal for grilling either under a domestic grill or outside over a barbecue. They don't take long, taste and look marvellous, and only need simple salads or boiled rice as an accompaniment.

There are certain rules, though. To flavour the meat or fish, and render it moist for the fierce heat of cooking, always marinate it first. The basics for marinades are lemon juice and olive oil, but add soy sauce, herbs (preferably fresh), crushed garlic, spices, wines, or use yoghurt or sour cream as a base instead. The longer food is left in the marinade, the more it absorbs flavours. Allow no more than 6 hours for fish, and up to 3 days for meat. Turn often in the marinade and dry thoroughly on kitchen paper before grilling.

Use beef, lamb, pork, liver, kidneys, chicken, turkeys, etc. for kebabs. Firm fish and scallops, prawns, shrimps and mussels are all good too. Intersperse the chunks on the skewers with onion, mushrooms, pieces of bacon, peppers, herb leaves, whatever you fancy.

Allow about 6-7 oz (175-200 g) of boned meat or fish per person. Baste with left-over marinade during cooking.

Serve with a selection of salads, or with the peas and chips. Kebabs go well with plain boiled rice, or with a rice pilaff (always pour any juices from grilling into the rice). You could do as the Greeks do, and serve the kebabs and salad in a sliced open *pitta* bread (good for a barbecue as no one needs a plate).

For 6 kebabs
about 2¼-2½ lb (1-1.1 kg) boned meat or fish, in chunks
about ½ pt (300 ml) marinade of choice
vegetables (see method), in chunks

Lamb Steaks

Serves 6

6 lamb steaks, weighing approxi-
    mately 7-8 oz (200-225 g) each

Marinade

6 tbsp olive oil
juice and grated rind of 2 lemons
1 tbsp ground coriander
salt and freshly ground black
    pepper
6 fresh sage leaves
3 tsp good runny honey

If it's too wet to barbecue, these steaks are delicious simply fried in butter.

Place the steaks in a flat container and pour the mixed marinade over, with a sage leaf on top of each steak. Cover and refrigerate for 2-3 days, taking the dish out of the fridge each morning and evening to turn the steaks, coating them liberally with the marinade. Just before barbecuing or frying remove steaks from the marinade and pat dry on kitchen paper.

If barbecuing, simply place on rack and keep your eye on it. If pan frying, coat the surface of your frying pan with oil, bring up to smoking point and then drop in 1 oz (25 g) butter. As the oil and butter get hot again, put only 2 of the steaks in the pan, and press down with a wooden spoon. Turn with the spoon as well.

2 minutes on each side will give you medium rare steaks;
3 minutes on each side for medium;
4 minutes on each side for well done;
5 minutes for charred burnt polystyrene!

Remove from frying pan and leave in warm oven. Cook the other steaks, 2 at a time, in the washed-out frying pan.

Chips in Newspaper

Serves 8

4 lb (1.8 kg) potatoes, peeled
fat for deep frying
sea salt
malt vinegar

If you have the luxury of an electric deep fryer chips are relatively simple to cook. I have one at home, but whenever I collect enough duck fat, I fry chips in a saucepan using a chip basket, as the flavour from the duck fat is superb. Beef dripping, too, is very fine for frying potatoes and if you ever cook turkey my way – in muslin, with loads of butter – all the lovely fat and butter left in the roasting tin is superb for frying chips.

When cutting chips do take a little care and time, making sure that your chips are all of similar size. Leave to soak in water.

Heat your fat to about 350°F (180°C). Dry the chips thoroughly on kitchen paper or a tea towel, and give them their first frying until nice and golden, then turn out onto kitchen paper. Just before you wish to serve the chips turn the fryer up to 375°F (190°C), then re-fry the chips for a few minutes to brown and crisp them.

Serve at once, liberally sprinkled with sea salt and a touch of malt vinegar – and why not serve them in a greaseproof paper lined newspaper wrapping? It'll add a touch of nostalgia...

Mushy Marrowfat Peas

Mushy marrowfat peas in my childhood were cheap and cheerful and 'good for you'. The local fish and chip shop would dollop them out into a mug you took with you – a dark green mess liberally laced with bicarbonate of soda to get that colour. They were eaten with the dark brown crispy chips and pennorth of bits.

When buying peas from your local health shop do always make sure they are sold with the special bicarbonate tablets, and follow the packet instructions carefully: without these magic morsels I am afraid marrowfat peas can be a disaster. I always soak mine for about 24 hours with the tablet: from rock-hard little bullets they will swell up proudly to a good chewy texture.

In Yorkshire, so says Pat Bridges, the traditional way is to cook the peas, after soaking, along with a skinned ham shank (which in its turn has been soaked to rid it of excess saltiness). A potato added to the cooking water takes up any residual saltiness (and must be discarded), and Sara Bridges insists that the mushy peas can't be eaten without a dollop of mint sauce.

I cook them in the following ways.

Drain the peas and wash and drain thoroughly again. Measure out 2 pt (a generous l) of cold water. Whichever flavouring you are using, add the soaked peas to the water along with the other ingredients, and simmer for 45-60 minutes, until they've become mushy.

Serves 8-10
1 lb (450 g) marrowfat peas, soaked
either *3 tablespoons dry English mustard*
8 oz (225 g) onions, finely chopped
or *a generous sprig fresh mint*
2 tablespoons runny honey

Rum Sultanas, Raisins and Currants in Puff Pastry

Roll puff pastry out to under ¼in (6mm) thickness, and cut into 12 large or 24 small squares.

To make the filling, beat the soft butter and brown sugar together until light and fluffy, then little by little beat in the rum. Mix the dried fruit and cinnamon together and fold into the rum butter.

Place a little of the fruit in the middle of each square. Beat the egg into the milk, and then paint around the edge of each square. Pull up each of the 4 corners to completely cover the filling, and press corners and sides gently shut. Turn over, place on greaseproof paper lined trays, paint with remaining wash if you like, and bake in a pre-heated oven set at 400°F (200°C), Gas 6 for about 15-20 minutes.

Makes 12 large or 24 small 'Eccles' cakes
1 lb (450 g) puff pastry
1 egg
¼ pt (150 ml) milk

Filling
2 oz (50 g) butter
2 oz (50 g) soft brown sugar
2 tbsp dark rum
2 oz (50 g) each of sultanas, raisins and currants
½ tsp cinnamon

Firework Barbecue

As this party will be mostly out of doors, once again a welcome arrangement will be ideal. On your porch or car port, or at the door leading into the garden, you will have an area from which to dispense drinks, so I have gone for the dramatic idea in the photograph between pages 120 and 121. I have chosen a tall black acrylic container – an umbrella stand – to support the blackened branch (in fact, a branch salvaged from a previous bonfire!). If you like the blackened idea – which does look good – you can spray a branch with matt spray paint (remember matt, not gloss). In the two places on the branch where I wished the arrangement to be, I attached a piece of dri-foam covered with cooking foil and sprayed matt black. Dried bracken ferns and clipped palmetto palm leaves – also black – are the main foliage pushed into the dri-foam, having first cut a slanting cut at the end of the stem. Scarlet pom-poms are dried flowers from the herbaceous plant Echinops (globe thistle), sprayed with a car lacquer paint in scarlet. The scarlet 'sparklers' are home-made and so easy – they are made of drinking straws, and when made are sprayed with the red paint as well.

1. *To make the straw sparklers, take about 12 straws and make them into a bunch – but not a neat one; keep them at irregular lengths. Take a florist's stub wire and pass it over the centre of the bunch of straws.*
2. *Bring the two ends down over the straws so that a large hair-pin shape is made. Push the straws in one direction and pull the 2 hair-pin wire legs in the other. This automatically fans the straws out into the sparkler shape. Twist the wire a couple of times under the straw sparkler and this then creates the stem. Cover the stem with florist's plastic stem tape and spray straws and stem with the scarlet paint.*

Branch
Bracken ferns
Palmetto palm leaves
Echinops heads
Straw 'sparklers'

Thanksgiving or Harvest Festival Lunch

Serves 6

Crudités with Herb Mayonnaise and Hot Spiced Cob
Cream of Mixed Vegetable Soup with Cinnamon Croûtons
Country Rabbit Casserole with Parisian Root Vegetables and Mashed Nut Potatoes
Pumpkin and Treacle Flan

Thanksgiving Day is a national holiday in the USA, celebrated on the fourth Thursday in November. It was originally observed by the Pilgrim Fathers, who, in 1621, celebrated their first – fairly meagre – harvest in North America. The turkeys traditionally eaten today by Americans are a reminder of the wild turkeys and venison given by the helpful local Indians. As turkeys are seldom found roaming wild in Great Britain – and are so central to our Christmas celebrations – I have made rabbit the centrepiece of this tasty and filling lunch. The pumpkin in the flan is another traditional American ingredient.

Harvest Home or Festival in Great Britain, generally celebrated earlier, in September or October, is a thanksgiving too for a successful farming year, and in tune with such a wealth of crops, the remainder of the recipes are designed to make full use of them.

Crudités with Herb Mayonnaise

radish flowers
celery twirls
strips of red pepper
turned mushrooms or peeled
    mushroom caps
lime baskets filled with turnip and
    carrot balls
paw paw strips
cucumber sticks or scored slices
generous sprigs of watercress
parsley and flowering herbs
    (particularly marjoram and
    borage)

Crudités are anything but 'crude', as they are fiddly and time-consuming to prepare and vanish in a few minutes when served with pre-dinner drinks. But they can be done in advance and add a touch of class to any party. You can of course just chop and section the vegetables into bite-size chunks, but it looks much more appealing if you take time to cut and trim and 'sculpt' your vegetables into beautiful shapes, as you would for a garnish. Arrange them on a platter, surrounding a central dish containing the mayonnaise.

The vegetables can be prepared earlier in the day, and provided they are totally covered with clingfilm and put in the fridge, come out beautifully fresh when needed.

Make your own mayonnaise for the dips, or buy large jars of the best commercial variety, and flavour it differently for each platter of crudités you intend to serve. Use tomato and garlic, mustard and honey, herbs, horseradish, chutney or curry powder.

Hot Spiced Cob

Per cob
1 oz (25 g) soft butter, mixed with
    crushed garlic and chopped
    herbs of choice

Use bought cob rolls for this recipe.

It's best if you are on your own when making the herb-garlic butter, as you can add and add, tasting as you go along, until you are satisfied with the flavour. Beat the chopped herbs – whatever are available – and as much garlic as you or your guests can stand, into the soft butter.

When you're happy, melt it gently in a saucepan. Make about 4 or 5 slits through the top crust of each cob down towards the base, but not right through. Take the base of the cob between the thumb and fingers of one hand and gently squeeze the 'cock's-comb' shape open. Paint liberally inside all the cut edges with the melted butter. Squeeze the cobs shut and wrap in individual pieces of foil.

When you wish to serve the cobs, simply place on a baking tray and heat through at 350°F (180°C), Gas 4 for about 12 minutes. Take out of oven and open the tops of foil on each cob and return to the oven for a further 5-8 minutes so that the tops become nice and crisp.

Cream of Mixed Vegetable Soup with Cinnamon Croûtons

Using up the leftover bits of the turned Parisian vegetables (see below), make up the weight to 2 lb (900 g) with more root vegetables, leeks, peas, outer cabbage and lettuce leaves, etc. They will all have to be chopped quite finely to match the small size of the root vegetable pieces.

Serves 6
2 lb (900 g) vegetables
4 oz (100-125 g) butter
8 oz (225 g) onions, finely chopped
¼ pt (150 ml) dry sherry
½ tsp salt and freshly ground black pepper
2 pt (a generous l) good stock

Melt the butter in a large saucepan, fry the onions until golden, and then add everything except the stock. As usual, cover the vegetables in the pan with a double piece of dampened greaseproof paper, put the lid on, and simmer gently for 40 minutes.

Add the stock and liquidize. Pass through a fine sieve into a clean pan. Heat through gently before serving.

Make the cinnamon croûtons by frying cubes of bread in butter and oil until brown. Sprinkle ground cinnamon over them in the pan, and serve in the soup with generous amounts of finely chopped parsley.

Country Rabbit Casserole

Divide the rabbits into portions. Remove flesh from bones of the ribcages, and cut and fold into small 'parcels'. Cut hind legs into two. Each shoulder makes 1 small portion. Coat each piece of rabbit in the seasoned wheatmeal flour, and seal 4 or 5 pieces at a time in the hot butter in a frying pan. Remove to a casserole. Deglaze the frying pan with the tarragon vinegar, and pour into the casserole. Finely chop the bacon, cook in washed frying pan until crisp, and put to one side.

Serves 6-8
3 rabbits, skinned
seasoned wheatmeal flour
4 oz (100-125 g) butter
1 dessertsp tarragon vinegar
8 rashers smoked bacon, minus rind
3 cloves of garlic, crushed
8 oz (225 g) onions, finely chopped
8 oz (225 g) carrots, thinly sliced
3 sticks celery, roughly chopped
4 oz (100-125 g) leeks, sliced
1 dessertsp brown sugar
½ pt (300 ml) red wine or cider
1 pig's trotter

Add the crushed garlic to the bacon fat in the pan, with the onions, carrot, celery and leeks. Fry until golden, then stir in the soft brown sugar. Place in the casserole with the rabbit. Pour over the wine or cider.

Brown the pig's trotter, cut into 3 or 4 pieces, in the oven preheated to 400°F (200°C), Gas 6, then add to casserole.

Cook the casserole at 350°F (180°C), Gas 4 for 1¼ hours and test the rabbit pieces with the sharp end of a knife. They should be lovely and tender, but occasionally they need a further 20 minutes.

Mashed Nut Potatoes

Serves 6

2 lb (900 g) potatoes, peeled and
    evenly cut
pinch of sea salt
1 egg, lightly beaten
4 tbsp double cream
2 oz (50 g) butter
7 oz (200 g) packet broken
    walnuts

Cover the potatoes with cold water, add sea salt, and bring to the boil. Reduce heat and simmer until potatoes are cooked, about 15 minutes. Strain well, dry out briefly over the heat, then mash well. When smooth, add the egg, double cream and butter and beat until light.

Crumble the broken walnuts up a bit more, and fold them into the smooth, creamy potatoes.

Parisian Root Vegetables

Serves 6

about 2 lb (900 g) each of carrots,
    turnips, parsnips
oil
butter
freshly ground black pepper

You may well think, initially, that this is a rather extravagant way to serve vegetables and you are quite right! But, of course, you do not throw away the balance; either cook and mash them for a supper dish, or use them as above, for a hearty home-made vegetable soup.

Peel the carrots (the larger the better), turnips and parsnips, and scoop out the balls. Don't worry if the balls aren't perfect — it's the effect on the plate that counts.

Throw the vegetable balls into a large saucepan of boiling salted water, bring back to the boil and cook for 2 minutes only. Quickly strain off the boiling water and then run cold water over the vegetables until they are quite cool. Pat dry and leave to one side.

When you wish to use them simply toss or stir-fry in a mixture of oil and butter for a few minutes. Be generous with the freshly ground black pepper just before serving.

Pumpkin and Treacle Flan

1 × 10in (25cm) cooked flan case
    (see page 54)
3 eggs
finely grated rind and juice of 2
    oranges
4 tbsp warmed golden syrup
2 oz (50 g) fine dried brown
    breadcrumbs
6 oz (175 g) pumpkin, very finely
    diced
ground cinnamon and ginger

Beat the eggs together with the juice and rind of the oranges. Mix in the warmed runny golden syrup, then fold in the breadcrumbs and diced pumpkin. Season with the cinnamon and ginger to personal taste.

Pour into the pre-cooked flan, and bake for 50 minutes at 350°F (180°C), Gas 4. Serve warm with whipped double cream, and garnish with pecan nut halves if you like.

Thanksgiving or Harvest Festival Lunch

Thanksgiving in America, Harvest Home in Britain – both are autumnal festivals to give thanks for a successful harvest, and what better time to investigate the decorative possibilities of fruit and vegetables? As you will have seen in many of my other arrangements throughout the book, I'm a great fan of the natural shapes and colours of fruit and vegetables. A look around any market stall or greengrocers will, if you're like me, inspire you with the sheer visual impact of much that's easily obtainable; haven't you ever longed to use the beauty of a cut-open red cabbage rather than just cook and eat it? I've created a welcome arrangement – see the photograph between pages 120 and 121 – inspired by the piles of fruit and vegetables that are heaped up in churches at Harvest Festival time, acknowledging also the influences of our trans-Atlantic neighbours – not many British farmers have yet achieved success with garlic, peppers, lemons and sweetcorn at this time of year!

When using fruit and vegetables a stem must be created, and this is best done with wooden skewers or wooden cocktail sticks, depending on the weight of the item used. Don't use wire, as it will damage the fruits or vegetables, which will then be uneatable after the arrangement is dismantled. I prepare everything in this way – carrots, corn on the cob, peppers etc.

As I wanted to have a harvesty, country look for this arrangement, I set up some American wooden buckets on the table (in the summer house in the photograph, but a porch or hall is the best place). As I also wanted them to look casual and cornucopia-like, the top bucket was filled with an old plastic bucket holding soaked floral foam. Into this I wedged a garden cane to support the spray of Spanish garlic. Tall straight leaves of the Yucca palm were then placed to give a bold firm foliage line, with Fatsia (japonica) leaves for boldness brought lower, and to the front. Sprays of blackberry foliage flow to the sides to soften the weight of the wooden buckets, and a cabbage was used for visual weight towards the base.

Marrows, red peppers, green chillies, lemons and a cut red cabbage are the main focal colour points in the group. I always say that in this type of arrangement you get colour, shapes, variety, texture, interest and a talking point – what else could anyone want?

Spray of Spanish garlic
Yucca palm leaves
Fatsia (*japonica*)
Blackberry
Cabbage
Marrows
Red peppers
Green chillies
Lemons
Red cabbage

Winter

Fruit

Apples · Chestnuts · Clementines · Cranberries · Dates · Lychees · Mandarins · Naartjes · Nuts · Pears · Pomegranates · Satsumas · Tangerines

Vegetables

Artichokes (globe and Jerusalem) · Broccoli · Brussels sprouts · Horseradish · Parsnips · Red cabbage · Spring greens · Turnips

Herbs

Rosemary · Winter Savory

Winter

Florist Flowers

Carnation (bloom and spray) · Chincherinchee (ornithogalum thyrsoides) · Chrysanthemum (bloom and spray) · Gerbera · Gladiolus · Lily · Rose

Garden Plant Materials

Evergreens

Buxus (Box) · Camellia · Cupressus (in many shades of green) · Eucalyptus (grey-greens) · Euonymus (spindle tree) · Fatsia · Hedera (Ivy) · Laurus (Laurel) · Mahonia · Picea (spruce) · Pinus (evergreen coniferous tree) · Pittosporum · Rhododendron · Yew (both green and golden)

Berries

Berberis · Cotoneaster · Fir cones of every shape and size · Hedera (berry clusters that spray well) · Holly · Pernettya · Pyracantha · Skimmia · Snowberry

Winter Food

I like winter, although I could be called a bit of a fraud as I escape from it to the warmth of South Africa! But I love the excitement of the run-up to Christmas, the heat inside contrasting with the cold outside, the hot rum toddy when coming in from shopping mid-morning, the decorations, the hot cup of chocolate with a dash of brandy and grated nutmeg before going to bed.

As I disappear just before Christmas, I do my usual MGM number much earlier than everyone else, decorating the house the last weekend in November. The trees are put into position, the coloured balls come out of their wrappings, the tree lights are lit (why, oh why is it that each year, between when you put them away, and then take them out again, about half of them stop working?). A few years ago I bought 500 or so artificial robins in Hong Kong (well, they were such a bargain), and for a while they festooned so many parts of the house that people actually ducked as they came up the stairs. They've dwindled in numbers over the years (perhaps they've flown back to the warmth of Hong Kong), but I still have a few on the tree in the car port.

Food is such fun at this time of year. The Christmas puddings will have been made earlier on – the recipe I give is a little extravagant, but so good – and the mincemeat too could be prepared well in advance. You could even make the mince pies; freeze them in the patty tins, then tip into polythene bags. When you want to eat them, pop back into patty tins and into the oven. Make apple sauce from the last of the windfalls, and lots of other things to go into the freezer and store cupboard. So that you have more time to spend with family and friends, have a big baking and cooking day when your kitchen will look as though the first winter storm has struck, and prepare flan bases, meringues, ice creams, casseroles, cakes, pâtés, etc. I also go at this time of year for the luxuries and winter tastes that make the cold bearable: foie gras, American red salmon caviare roe, hand-made chocolates, the nuts, raisins, marshmallows, home-made truffles and toffees, and the wonderful tangerines and satsumas. Just thinking about it all makes me long for winter again – but at the same time I'm glad, for my figure's sake, that I do escape!

Obviously turkey must appear at this time of year, but if you're reluctant to jade your palate with turkey with everything, I hope my idea might please you. Or you could do as more and more people are doing, and serve something completely different; the Americans have their turkey at Thanksgiving, and serve prime roast ribs of beef or goose at Christmas.

The other winter occasions are a New Year or Hogmanay party, a St Valentine's dinner for romantics, and a brunch – one of my favourite meals of the day.

Winter Flowers

Autumn is now over and we are coming into the colder months. It is the anticipation of Christmas and the preparation of the baubles and bangles and beads that occupy my mind and fingers at this time. It is never too early to start to prepare your Christmas materials. Spray painting, for instance, is something that can be done well in advance, and the plant or whatever can dry happily away, waiting, ready to be built into your arrangements. In any spare moment, I pick through my boxes and piles of stuff in the attic and spare room, hunting out things I'd forgotten, or things that could be transformed for use this year. I love these months and weeks before Christmas!

Most of the garden flowers have finished, but there are still some berries and shrubs that can be picked. There are all the evergreens, of course, and my favourite berries, and these, together with the glycerined foliage you prepared in the autumn (see page 101), can form the start of any arrangement.

There are two plants in particular that I should like to concentrate on. To keep holly berries for Christmas you can – as I once heard – prevent the birds stealing them by threading old pairs of tights over the branches! My imagination works overtime whenever I visualize an intrepid climber, and what the tree looks like after this treatment! My way is simpler and better. At the beginning of December, or whenever you think best, pick sprays of holly berries and place them on a sheet of plastic. Cover the sprays with a second sheet of plastic and a heavy sack or old blanket. Weight the edges with stones. It will look like a large Cornish pastry, and take up a lot of space, but at least it keeps the birds off and the berries will have swollen in size by the time you need them.

The other plant is the Poinsettia (euphorbia pulcherrima), the Christmas flower par excellence. We see these mainly in pot-plant form, which, if well cared for, will last for weeks. Not many people know this, but the actual flower of the poinsettia is composed of the insignificant bobbles in the centre; the conspicuous bracts with a petal-like appearance surrounding the flower are part of the foliage. Poinsettias come in various colours – white, cream, pink, apricot and, of course, the very popular red – and they can be very successfully used in the centre of an arrangement still in their pots. The stems can also be cut from the poinsettia plant and used in the centre of a large arrangement, or one or two heads can be used in a simple modern arrangement. The thing to remember about the poinsettia when cut is that it produces a white milky substance. This seepage must be stopped by burning and sealing with a match or candle. Plunge the cut flowers thereafter, in the usual way, into deep cold water for 12 hours, before using in your arrangement.

Christmas Lunch or Dinner

Serves 6-8

Chestnut Soup with Diced Red Peppers and Deep-fried Parsley

Smoked Haddock and Pea Cream Quiche

Baked Breast of Turkey

New Potatoes, Broad Beans and Broccoli Florets

Christmas Pudding with Brandy Cream

Lemon Mincemeat

This most important day of the year is one you want to spend with your family and friends – and not up to your eyes in pots, pans, dishes and food in the kitchen. The Christmas meal should be as relaxing and pleasant for the cook/host as for the guests, and so almost everything in this party menu can be prepared well in advance. The pudding and mincemeat have been ready for weeks (if not months), the soup can be made the day before, and you could have taken the base for the quiche out of the freezer. The turkey can be ready in its foil wrapping just to be put in the oven when the time comes. Even the vegetables could have been prepared the day before; peeled and cut they will come to no harm stored in jars of lightly salted water somewhere cool for 24 hours.

I once spent Christmas Day at a health farm in the wine-growing area of the Cape. Some sympathetic friends brought champagne and mince pies. They were delicious after a diet of nothing but hot vegetable tea and the occasional slice of paw-paw, but the champagne went to my head! Never again will I so deprive myself at Christmas – I'll save the dieting for later, perhaps in mid-January, and then maybe I'll fit my clothes again!

Chestnut Soup with Diced Red Peppers and Deep-fried Parsley

Be sure that all the vegetables are cut in even-sized pieces. Melt the butter in a saucepan, add the onions, and sauté slowly until golden. Add the other vegetables, with the wine, salt and pepper and chestnut purée. Cover the vegetables with a double thickness of dampened greaseproof paper, and then put on the lid. Simmer on a low heat for 40 minutes.

Add stock and liquidize in 2 or 3 batches, and then pass through a fine sieve into a clean saucepan. Check the seasoning and serve hot with the red pepper, cut into small dice, as a garnish along with the deep-fried sprigs of parsley.

Deep-fried Parsley

Always use a large sprig of parsley for each bowl, as it shrivels when deep fried. Heat the fat in the deep fryer to 365°F (184°C), and check the parsley over for any little bits of dirt. Arrange the large pieces of parsley on the base of the deep frier basket and just before you actually dish up the soup, submerge in the pre-heated oil. There will be an immediate sizzle and the fat will go frothy, but in a matter of seconds, this action will cease and the parsley is ready. Drain well before using.

Serves 8

8 oz (225 g) onions, finely diced
8 oz (225 g) leeks, cleaned and diced
8 oz (225 g) potatoes, peeled and diced
4 oz (100-125 g) butter
¼ pt (150 ml) dry white wine
½ tsp salt
freshly ground black pepper
1 lb (450 g) unsweetened chestnut purée
1½ pt (900 ml) good chicken stock
1 large red pepper, for garnish
parsley

Smoked Haddock and Pea Cream Quiche

Finely flake the boneless smoked haddock with the nutmeg and the 2 tbsp double cream. Arrange in the flan in circles, starting from the outside of the cooked flan, leaving room for alternate circles of the pea purée.

Liquidize the cooked peas with the egg and sugar and then pipe this mixture in between the smoked haddock circles. The final effect will be like a pool into which a stone has been thrown with rings emanating from the centre (see photograph between pages 144 and 145).

Mix together the custard ingredients, pour over the contents of the flan case, and bake in a pre-heated oven at 375°F (190°C), Gas 5 for 35 minutes.

You can use spinach purée instead of the peas if you like, and a touch of grated Cheddar cheese with the haddock is tasty.

Serves 8

1 × 10in (20cm) pre-cooked flan base (see page 54)
6 oz (175 g) filleted smoked haddock
generous pinch nutmeg
2 tbsp double cream
4 oz (100-125 g) cooked peas
1 egg
½ tsp sugar

Custard

½ pt (300 ml) double cream
2 eggs
1 egg yolk
salt and freshly ground black pepper

Baked Breast of Turkey

Serves 8

1 half turkey
1 lb (450 g) butter
3 cloves garlic, crushed with
*   1 tsp salt*
1 tsp dried rosemary
chopped parsley or chives
freshly ground black pepper

To many people all that left-over turkey is sheer anathema, so, if like me, turkey rissoles, turkey curry, turkey vol-au-vents and turkey risotto (all within the space of a few days) don't appeal, try my solution to the problem. Get together with a like-minded friend, and share a 16-17 lb (roughly 7-7.5 kg) turkey. Ask your butcher to simply cut the fresh turkey straight through its breast bone on his band-saw, then each family has a breast, which will give a generous 6 portions, and the leg, boned and rolled, will give at least enough for another 3 portions.

It is a relatively simple task to remove the breast meat and wing from the ribcage in one whole piece. Bone, roll and tie the leg.

Mix the butter with the garlic and rosemary, and melt about half of it. Have ready two pieces of foil, one large enough to completely enclose the breast, and one for the rolled leg. Paint the foil with the melted butter, place the turkey portions on top, and smear with the rest of the butter. Put in the parsley or chives, or both, and sprinkle with plenty of pepper. Fold the foil over the turkey, and seal so that they look like huge Cornish pasties.

When you wish to cook, simply pre-heat oven to 400°F (200°C), Gas 6, put parcels on a roasting tray and bake for 1¼ hours.

New Potatoes

Serves 6-8

1¼ lb (550 g) new potatoes
1½ pt (850 ml) water
salt
4 tsp chopped fresh herbs or
*   2 tsp dried*
4 oz (100-125 g) butter

Sometimes new potatoes from far-off places can be found around Christmas, and they make a delicious change from roast.

Scrub potatoes lightly under cold running water with a scouring pad (needless to say a clean, not soapy, one). Place in a saucepan and cover with the water. Use less salt than you would normally add to taste, along with the chopped fresh herbs or dried mixed herbs and butter.

All you do is bring the water with the potatoes to the boil and cook until all the water has evaporated; this takes about 20 minutes.

Broccoli Florets

Fresh broccoli is seen more and more throughout the year, but I sometimes find the large bits are a bit tough in the stem when the flowery ends are over-cooked. Try this method of cooking them to solve the problem.

Painstakingly cut the broccoli into individual small florets and chuck the stalks into the stock pot. These small florets are then quickly cooked in boiling salted water for just 1 minute and left to one side.

When you wish to serve them, heat them through quickly in a small frying pan in walnut oil. Sprinkle them generously with the ground coriander.

Serves 6-8
3-4 lb (1.4-1.8 kg) broccoli
salt
1 tbsp (or more) walnut oil
ground coriander

Broad Beans

One of my favourite vegetables, and well worth all the hard slog. It is good to see them available in the shops during winter, coming in from sunny Spain.

This quantity of podded beans will yield about 1 lb, 5 oz (600 g) when taken out of the pods after cooking.

Place the pods in a pan of lightly salted cold water, bring to the boil and cook for 1 minute only. Remove immediately, strain off hot water and then refresh beans under a cold running tap.

Now the fag begins. Take each cooked bean between your thumb and forefinger with the shoot end exposed. Gently tear this end open and by exerting a little pressure on the pod, the beautiful smooth green beans will literally pop out. These are what you use, and you must discard the pods. (It will take you about 15-20 minutes, I'm afraid.)

When you wish to serve them, simply warm the beans through in milk, water or chicken stock, but do not over-cook or over-heat at this stage.

Serves 6
3 lb (1.4 kg) broad beans
milk, water or chicken stock

Christmas Pudding

Makes 4 × 1½ pt (900 ml) puddings

First Stage

8 oz (225 g) each of currants and seedless raisins
4 oz (100-125 g) muscatels
6 oz (175 g) sultanas
4 oz (100-125 g) glacé cherries, rinsed and roughly chopped
4 oz (100-125 g) dried apricots, diced
4 oz (100-125 g) mixed glacé fruit, diced (if you can get it, use that from the Cape: it's not so sweet)
2 oz (50 g) each of preserved ginger, candied orange and citron peel, roughly chopped
½ pt (300 ml) dry sherry
½ pt (300 ml) cooking brandy
2 tsp pure glycerine (from good chemists)

Second Stage

8 oz (225 g) white breadcrumbs
5 oz (150 g) plain flour
1 tsp each of salt, baking powder, ground cinnamon and mace
½ tsp mixed spice
pinch of ground ginger
4 oz (100-125 g) soft butter
4 oz (100-125 g) each of shredded suet, white sugar and demerara sugar
4 oz (100-125 g) shelled almonds, chopped
4 oz (100-125 g) carrots, grated
8 oz (225 g) apples, peeled and cored
5 eggs, lightly beaten
2 tbsp golden syrup
1 tsp black treacle

The puddings can be made in October, and stored in a well-ventilated dry place. They taste all the better for this maturing! As you can see from the photograph between pages 144 and 145 it does call for a lot of ingredients, but all your effort is well worthwhile.

The puddings should be made in stages. You could double the ingredients and make 8 puddings instead of 4. This may sound extravagant, but I give them, beautifully wrapped, as Christmas presents to my friends – and while I am barbecuing on Christmas Day in some tropical clime, I can be sure they're thinking of me!

First Stage

Two days before you intend cooking the pudding, soak the dried fruit ingredients in the booze. Put them all in a large basin and pour in the sherry, brandy and glycerine. Mix well, cover and leave, stirring occasionally.

Second Stage

On the day of cooking, mix the breadcrumbs with the plain flour, salt, baking powder, cinnamon, mace, mixed spice and ground ginger. Gently rub in the soft butter, and then add the shredded suet, the sugars, the chopped almonds and grated carrot. Coarsely grate the apples straight into the mixture. Add the soaked fruit and any juices.

Bring it all together with the 5 lightly beaten eggs mixed with the warmed golden syrup and black treacle. Mix well to distribute all the ingredients evenly. It is very sticky!

Portion out into the greased bowls. Cut circles of double thickness greaseproof paper and press these down on top of the puddings. Cover with damp circles of muslin or old sheets and overlap the sides so that you can firmly tie them on with string. Sprinkle a generous amount of flour on top of this damp secure cloth.

Place the pudding basins into a deep roasting tray, and pour in enough boiling water to come halfway up the roasting tray. Cover this completely with foil. 'Steam' in a pre-heated oven at 350°F (180°C), Gas 4 for 3½-4 hours. Turn off oven and leave puddings in to cool. Store covered with fresh greaseproof, foil or cloth in a cool dry place.

When you want to serve them they are reheated similarly, and take 1½ hours to come round to edible temperature.

Brandy Cream

Having such a sumptuous Christmas pud you can't be mean with the sauce – and anyway the puddings themselves will have come out of the October budget!

1 pt (600 ml) double cream
3 tbsp cooking brandy
3 tbsp caster sugar

Reduce the double cream by half, and then beat in the brandy and sugar. Serve immediately with the wedge of pudding.

You can also serve brandy or rum butter, which is particularly delicious if you have any cold pudding left over.

Lemon Mincemeat

The addition of lemon juice and rind to mincemeat makes for an interesting mince pie with a bit of a bite to it – something people are looking for at the end of a rich meal. The mincemeat should be made 2-3 weeks before being used, and this too makes a good Christmas present, like the Christmas puddings.

Makes about 6 lb (2.7 kg)
4 lemons
1 lb (450 g) beef suet
1 lb (450 g) currants
1 lb (450 g) demerara sugar
¾ lb (350 g) soft sponge cake, crumbled
¾ lb (350 g) candied peel
¾ lb (350 g) nibbed almonds
¼ pt (150 ml) sherry
¼ pt (150 ml) cooking brandy

Finely grate the rind from the lemons and then squeeze out the juice. Crumble the beef suet finely, and then simply mix all the ingredients together in a large bowl. Spoon out into immaculately clean warm jam jars and pack it in tightly. Cover with greaseproof paper circles and then add cellophane tops held in place with elastic bands.

Use in steamed puddings, with puff pastry for pies, or in open tarts, as well as in the traditional mince pies.

Christmas Lunch or Dinner

Welcome Ring

Metal or plastic ring
Ribbon
Holly
Wax roses
Pine cones
Wicker bells

Christmas is the time of year that everyone loves, no matter what age, and I make absolutely no excuses for the length of this section, and the number of ideas I suggest. I love Christmas! I think that your welcome signs should start right at the door. Even before the guests have pressed the bell what could be better than a welcoming door ring (not wreath, please don't call it that).

Buy either a metal or plastic ring from a florist's shop, and this then can be tackled in various ways, depending upon the finished effect you want. You could, for instance, bind the frame with colourful 1in (2.5cm) wide ribbon, keeping the ribbon flat and neat as you go, securing it at the back with sticky tape. Then you can fix on a piece of dri-foam, about 2in (5cm) square, again with sticky tape, and into this one area, you make your arrangement (rather like the autumn ring on page 113). Use leaves, cones, berries, fruits, etc. and a bow of ribbon.

For my Christmas ring (photograph between pages 144 and 145) I have used holly because of its lasting qualities out of water, although I do condition the holly sprays for about 3 days before using (see page 133). The pieces of holly were cut into 4in (10cm) lengths and bound onto the frame with florist's reel wire. Lay one holly piece at a time onto the frame, bind round a couple of times with the wire, and continue until the frame is neatly covered. Wax Christmas roses bought from the local florist's shop were then twisted into the holly.

The pine cones in the arrangement need stems before they can be placed, and this is easy. Take the cone in one hand and a piece of florist's stub wire in the other, and force the wire around and into the row of scales nearest to the cone's bottom end. Only take the wire halfway round the cone, and then bring the 2 ends of the wire together over the base of the cone (where the natural stem would have been). Twist the 2 wire legs together, thus creating a stem. As with the wax Christmas roses, twist the wire leg into the holly. To give colour to the ring there cannot be anything better than red ribbon. I have used water-repellent velvet, but any water-resistant ribbon will do. Make your bow as described on page 145, and then attach its wire stem to the ring, together with, in this case, three wicker bell shapes. You could use bought Christmas tree decorations, but a very cheap bell effect can be obtained by spraying small plastic plant pots with spray paint, securing them onto the ring by a wire pushed through the drainage holes in the bottom.

To hang the ring, fix a piece of ribbon to match the bow to the top of the ring and take the ribbon up over the door top. Staple or drawing-pin it on to the thickness of the door; pushing the pins home well so that the door will shut properly in its frame. Not

only is this method of hanging good for the door (you don't want holes in the woodwork), but it's also a very good idea for those doors that open straight onto the pavement. Rather than detaching the ring every night to counter an unseasonal dishonesty, you can swing the ring over the door top to hang inside. Every morning when you bring the milk in, swing the ring over the top and outside again. Simple, isn't it!

Christmas Welcome Arrangement

The next welcome arrangement should be in the hallway. The old oak chest in my hall that holds the welcome arrangement in the photograph between pages 144 and 145 was cleared of an accumulation of things so that I had a good clear space on which to work.

I am a lover of foliage, fruits and berries, as you may have realized by now! I like them all in one massed arrangement, so the 'container' I chose gives, I think, this massed effect as well as looking rather like a yule log. It could so easily be put together by any handy person given the right materials, but I bought mine ready made. A slice of olive wood begged from a wood yard in southern Spain forms the base. Attached to this is a half log to give weight, and then attached to this in turn is a solid branch with an interesting shape. Affixed to the branch in 3 positions are cork bark containers, complete circles of cork bark about 9in (22.5cm) in diameter, and about 5in (12.5cm) deep; into these I put plastic containers to hold the soaked floral foam (about half the foliage is natural).

Although I have 3 groups in the arrangement, the whole must be treated as one. The height of the arrangement and some of the width is created by sprays of a lovely blue cedar (cedrus). Don't be scared of going fairly high with the top pieces and have a nice generous flow to the sides. To thicken the outline, and still keeping to fresh plant material, I have used a variegated holly (ilex aquifolium 'aureo medio picta'). There are other beautiful variegated hollies such as Golden Milkboy or Golden Milkmaid, some very slow growing, but well worth having. Do also look out for the silver varieties at your local nurseries; ilex (aquifolium 'argentea-marginata'), with its silver margins, is a very good one.

Now that we have the basic outline we can start to increase the visual weight. I found some very lovely sprays of polyester vine and variegated ivy, and they fitted in well. Some sneaky pruning of an indoor plant – nephrolepis fern – gave me another shape. At this stage the central positioning of the fruit should be considered as this has to be well anchored. The fresh pineapples with wooden skewers in the bottom end to act as a stem are the first placements, followed by large, well polished rosy apples, and bunches of black grapes. The bunches of grapes again have to be well anchored, so I wire a wooden skewer to the stem.

Branch and base
Cedar
Holly
Polyester vine and ivy
Nephrolepis fern
Pineapples
Apples
Grapes
Artificial berries and fruits
Pine cones
Ivy
Philodendron
Lotus seed pods

141

Sprays of artificial berries and fruits were then brought into each of the 3 groupings, together with natural pine cones.

To bring the centre of each group together some large foliage was needed. I could have gone for a large variety of ivy, but because I wanted a warmer richer colour I chose some treated philodendron leaves, which were dyed a subtle shade of burgundy. I added lotus seed pods, with their holey middles, to keep the woody effect going through the group. When I thought that the arrangement was just about finished, I added some sprays of creamy berries from Japan to soften the outline.

Garlands

Garland base (see method)
Foliage (cupressus, box, yew, holly)
Pine cones
Wax roses
Lacquered fruits
Ribbon bows

Garlands of leaves and flowers were made for all sorts of reasons throughout history and all over the world, so what better for Christmas than a garland to greet your friends and relations – which could, of course, be draped across the frame of your front door instead of the welcome ring. The garland in the photograph between pages 144 and 145 drapes over a brass butcher's pole above my stone fireplace, looking cheerful, and creating a warm, seasonal cosiness.

The basic idea is simple, but the permutations are endless. A garland can be made in various ways, and one of the best is with a base of tubular polythene and floral foam. Soak the floral foam and cut the larger blocks lengthways. When completely soaked let it drain for a few moments, then push into the plastic tubing. After each piece has been put in the tube, tie string round, and you will end up with what looks like a string of sausages! This ensures that the garland will bend naturally. This method of garland making is best if you want to use fresh flowers and foliage, but if you make it fairly long it does get rather heavy.

Once you've made the sausage string, cover your working surface with plastic sheeting if it needs protection from scratches or water (I always work at a work-bench in the garage). Having well prepared your foliage and flowers, cut them into 4-5in (10-12.5cm) pieces. As always, cut the stems with a slanting cut to create a point that will be easy to push through the plastic tube into the soaked foam. If you find that some stems won't go through the plastic, just make a hole with a metal meat skewer and then push in the flower or foliage. Make sure that you push the foliage in at an angle, overlaying each time so that no plastic will be seen when the garland is finished.

Make your garland the day before you want to hang it in its final position, and hang it up in the garage, or wherever, to allow water that may seep through holes to do its seeping where it doesn't matter (anything's better than on your living-room carpet).

Another way of garland making – and very simple and effective it is too – is to use an old washing line, and wire the flowers and foliage to it. Obviously there will be no water to refresh the plant *material in a garland of this sort, but as long as you condition your material well – giving it a couple of days' watering before use – it will last well. Cut the foliage into 4-5in (10-12.5cm) lengths. Cupressus, box, yew and, of course, holly all last well out of water. Again prepare the garland where you don't mind a mess. I do this in the garage, knocking a large nail into the work bench and tying the washing line around the nail. I then bind my various pieces of prepared foliage on to the line with florist's reel wire. This way you can just go on forever working backwards without having to support the weight of the plastic tubing. This garland could also be prepared a couple of weeks before Christmas and kept in a large plastic bag; just give it a splash of water every other day or so.*

Hang the garland in position first and then attach the wired pine cones, wax Christmas roses and lacquered fruits to give colour and interest. I finished off the garland in the photograph with large bows of velvet ribbon at the point where the sweep and the fall of the garland met. Hanging off the end of the garland drops are large pine cones (the ones used in the Hanging Cone idea). A bell shape once again would look good at the end of the garlands.

Christmas Tree

I think Christmas trees look best – like most flower arrangements – if a particular colour scheme is chosen and adhered to. I have chosen a red colour scheme for my tree, using various tones of red, and even red gingham ribbons. There are red lacquered fruits and berries, red false paper-covered parcels with green strings (you could tie up tiny presents like mini fruit and nut packets), red baskets full of red paper-covered sweets, with red and gingham bows, interspersed with natural pine cones. Do try to make it look as full and exciting as possible. Add lights if you want; you should be able to get them in sets of just one colour to match your scheme. I also suggest you keep the bigger presents to the base of the tree and then your tree isn't spoiled when the raiding starts on Christmas morning!

The Dining Table

Having now decorated the house for the guests to arrive, from the front door to the log fire, only the dining table is left. Because my carved oak table is so beautiful, it would have been sacrilege to cover the wood with a cloth, so I chose gold place mats to be the basic link with the tall church candlesticks (see photograph between pages 144 and 145).

I stand these well-loved candlesticks on brass plates from Morocco for more impact and visual weight. To adapt a candlestick to hold flowers, you can buy candlecup holders made of plastic or of metal to match your candlestick (available in different coloured metals). I prefer the metal because they keep their shape better. The cup holders are shaped like a scoop with a protruding piece at the

Candles
Nephrolepis fern
Hawthorn berries
Lacquered berries
Holly
Spray carnations and carnations
Grapes
Apples
Tangerines
Ribbon bows
Roses ('Mercedes')

143

bottom, which goes into the hole where the candle normally sits. I put a ring of plasticine around the protruding piece first, which gives a kind of suction, keeping the holder in place. I then put a piece of floral foam into the scoop and anchor it across the top with floral foam tape.

The first placement is the candle, with its tripod of wooden cocktail sticks, which go astride the floral foam tape. Never forget to work both arrangements at the same time. The outline was, as always, the first consideration, and I used some sprays of the lovely delicate nephrolepis fern. Sprays of hawthorn berries were also used in the outline because they hang so well. These were picked a few weeks before and left in the garden under plastic sheeting. These berries are a very dark red colour and tend to look rather dark and dull, so I made up some sprays of shining red lacquered berries to be more of a highlight. Variegated holly was the next placement, on both sides of each arrangement, using it both for its colour and as a bolder foliage to help hide the floral foam.

Once I was satisfied that the shape of each arrangement was to my liking I then divided the flower plant material in half so that each arrangement would have the same number of flowers. To start with I used red spray carnations, nicely flowing from each side towards the centre, following the shape already created with the foliage and berries. If any fruit is to be used, it should go in now. Grapes cascade from either side at the centre, having wired a cocktail stick onto the stem first. Polished apples and small tangerines were also included, these too with wooden cocktail stick stems. I wanted to have some ribbon bows in the groups, and instead of the obvious red velvet I chose a more subtle, open-worked mulberry colour edged in fine gold thread, with a small gold bow in the centre. My next flowers were red carnations, followed by one of my favourite small size commercial roses, 'Mercedes'. The two candlesticks were then put on the table and viewed from every place setting so that there were no obvious gaps or mechanics showing.

The next stage with the table layout is to put the place mats and cutlery in place so that you can gauge how much room will be left for any further arrangements. Having created the height with the candlesticks, it's visually effective to balance that height with a lower arrangement, to bring the plant materials down onto the table. The island on which the central arrangement sits is an oval shape covered in red velvet and edged in green braid (see page 76 for instructions on how to make). A low plastic dish holds the soaked floral foam, this time taking a group of three centrally placed candles. Never rely on just a couple of candles for light at your table, you'll have your guests groping for their spoons, wondering what on earth they have on their plates. Always have plenty of candlelight (which supposedly flatters women – but what does it do for fellers?). To get the candles at slightly different heights, I used

*A Christmas welcome arrangement in the hall using an unusual
'container' and three separate groupings of fresh and artificial materials.
The family Christmas presents displayed alongside are almost a
decoration in themselves!*

Previous Page. *Your Christmas decorations should start right at the front
door, with a ring bedecked with holly, wax Christmas roses, pine cones,
wicker bells and a red velvet bow.*

Left. *Serve a slice of the unusual and colourful smoked haddock and pea cream quiche as the second course of the delicious Christmas lunch or dinner.*

Below. *Turkey is traditional in Britain, of course, but try this less usual way of preparing it. Bake the breast in foil with lots of herby butter.*

*Continue your Christmas welcome (above and opposite, below) with hanging garlands,
a sophisticated tree, and a superb table setting, with three flower arrangements, candles, and crackers.
The photographs were taken in Derek Bridges' hill-top home.*

Left. *An icy arrangement for New Year, to match the snow and ice outside – made from plastic snowflake-shaped discs, glass bells and home-made sugared almond flowers.*

Start a lazy winter brunch with a helping of extravagant but healthy muesli, and follow later with creamy scrambled eggs and smoked salmon bits.

the cocktail stick tripod on one and three longer wooden meat skewers on the other two.

As with the candlesticks I wanted a flowing arrangement to each long side and, of course, I had to use the same plant material. But I did want more fruit, so after the outline materials of nephrolepis ferns and berries were placed, I decided to have a cascade of fruits flowing across the arrangement centre. Grapes, tangerines, peaches and apples were all mounted on cocktail sticks and arranged across the container. The same ribbon bows as on the candlesticks were placed into the arrangement and then I could concentrate on the flowers. Spray carnations following the line of the foliage were placed in, the outside ones flowing down towards the base, and then the red carnations and 'Mercedes' red roses. Pieces of variegated holly were tucked between the central flowers and fruits to soften the round shapes of the fruit. Never, even in a bowl of fruit, just have all those shapes without some softening effect. A piece of soaked floral foam in film with some foliage pushed in works wonders.

The table arrangement is now almost complete. Green Wedgwood leaf plates were used on the table to pick up the greens of the foliage, red napkins folded on each side plate carried on the red and green theme, as do gold and scarlet crackers, one for each guest, with a gold name-tag on each.

Bow Tying

Many people ask me how much ribbon it takes to make a bow, which of course is a difficult question to answer, as it all depends on how big a bow you want to make! Whatever size of bow, though, the method is the same. Start with a container of ribbon, rather than a pre-cut length, and never cut your ribbon until at the last stage.

1. *To make a bow with 4in (10cm) petals or loops, pinch the ribbon between the forefinger and thumb of one hand 4in (10cm) from the end. Make a loop 4in (10cm) long with the other hand and pinch together between the forefinger and thumb. Keep going with the ribbon across the forefinger and thumb, pinching the same length of ribbon each time you cross the centre, until it looks a little like an old-fashioned aircraft propeller. Make 3 loops on either side of the finger and thumb, 6 loops in all, and cut off the surplus ribbon, leaving another 4in (10cm) tail.*
2. *Still holding all the ribbon loops in the fingers, take a piece of florist's stub wire and put it across where you have been holding the ribbon. Push the wire downwards, trapping the ribbon in the rounded head of a long hair-pin. Push the petals upwards and twist the wire stems down, and together, creating the stem, and trapping the loops in the wire.*
3. *Put a finger into each loop and pull into shape.*

New Year Dinner

Serves 8

Kipper and Lemon Pâté with Horseradish Cream

Pot Roast Beef with Vegetables

Apple Sponge Slice with Honey Yoghurt

So often at this time of the year people's purses are empty and their bellies full with the excesses of Christmas, so I was torn between inventing a very simple calorie-free meal and a meal appropriate to the occasion and the weather. Then I thought 'What the hell, this is supposed to be a fun book', so the following menu resulted.

The kipper and lemon pâté – the only thing which remotely relates to the essential Scottishness of Hogmanay – is delicious by itself, but I have also used it with eggs· half fill the ramekins with the pâté, top it off with hot buttered chive-herb eggs. The pot roast is simple to cook and very rich, and as I throw in so many vegetables you only need some creamed potatoes as accompaniment. The baked apple sponge slice, the only thing that needs to be cooked the evening of the party, is served with natural yoghurt instead of the usual cream or egg custard.

The kipper pâté recipe can easily be doubled and frozen, and you will have some of the beef left for the following day (saves you cooking after all that celebrating).

Kipper and Lemon Pâté with Horseradish Cream

This pâté is simplicity itself to make if you have a good liquidizer or processor. If you haven't either, then I can't suggest how you do it apart from beating everything vigorously with an electric beater or, worse still, by hand!

Put the boned, skinned kipper fillets in the processor with the cheese, 2 oz (50 g) of the soft butter, lemon juice and rind, parsley, horseradish cream and pepper, and whizz around for several minutes until lovely and smooth.

Spoon out into small individual dishes and flatten. Meanwhile slowly melt the remaining butter and when cool and settled, strain off the clarified butter, leaving the scum behind. Pour this gently over the dishes of pâté and chill in the fridge. Garnish with a wedge of tomato and a leaf or two of parsley. Serve with hot toast and butter.

Serves 8
12 oz (350 g) boned, skinned kipper fillets
4 oz (100-125 g) cream cheese
10 oz (275 g) soft butter
juice and grated rind of 1 lemon
1 tbsp finely chopped parsley
1 tbsp horseradish cream
freshly ground black pepper

Pot Roast Beef with Vegetables

This dish is best cooked in a large heat- and oven-proof casserole with a close-fitting lid (or you can use a doubled thickness of foil as a lid). If you prefer the dish to be slightly spicy, simply add ¼ tsp of allspice and ¼ tsp of curry powder to the flour when thickening.

Seal the meat on all sides in 2 oz (50 g) of the butter in a frying pan. Remove and put meat in casserole. Cut the carrots, turnips and parsnips to roughly the same size and shape and brown in remaining fat, adding more if necessary. Remove and put alongside the meat. Fry the button onions, then the chopped onions and garlic, remove to the casserole, then deglaze the frying pan with the stock and red wine. Add to the meat and vegetables in the casserole along with the bay leaves.

Cook in pre-heated oven at 350°F (180°C), Gas 4 for 2½ hours. Remove from oven and transfer meat and vegetables to a separate dish, leaving gravy behind. Beat together the remaining butter with the plain flour to make a paste. Put casserole on the burner and little by little beat in balls of the paste to thicken the juices. Cook for about 5 minutes on top of stove, then return meat and vegetables to casserole and put back in oven for a further 30 minutes.

Serve simply with mounds of buttery, creamy, creamed potatoes.

Serves 8
rolled sirloin of beef, about 4 lb (1.8 kg)
3 oz (75 g) butter
6 oz (175 g) each of carrots, turnips and parsnips, peeled
6 oz (175 g) button onions, peeled, topped and tailed
8 oz (225 g) onions, finely chopped
2 cloves garlic, crushed with a pinch of salt
¼ pt (150 ml) beef stock
¼ pt (150 ml) red wine
2 bay leaves
1 oz (25 g) plain flour

Apple Sponge Slice with Honey Yoghurt

Serves 8

4 Granny Smith apples
8 tbsp cider
butter
3 oz (75 g) caster sugar
2 eggs, lightly beaten
4 oz (100-125 g) self-raising flour
milk
icing sugar
½ pt (300 ml) natural yoghurt
2 tbsp warm runny honey

Peel the apples, cut in half through the equator and take out the centre. Place these 8 apple halves flat side down on a greased baking tray with a lip, and pour 1 tbsp cider over each half. Bake in a pre-heated oven at 350°F (180°C), Gas 4 for 15 minutes until just starting to cook.

Meanwhile lightly butter an oval cooking dish and make the batter. Cream 3 oz (75 g) butter and the sugar together and little by little beat in the lightly beaten eggs. Carefully fold in the sieved self-raising flour, and add a little cold milk to obtain a dropping consistency.

Arrange the partly cooked apples in the buttered oval dish, flat side down. Pour the batter mixture over them, and put back in the oven at the same temperature for a further 45 minutes.

To serve, remove from oven, dust with icing sugar, take to the table and serve with the natural yoghurt mixed with the warm runny honey.

New Year Dinner

The party season is coming to an end but it's not quite Twelfth Night yet, so some of your Christmas decorations will still be in place. You may not feel inclined to do fresh flower arrangements for a New Year Party, but there are other possibilities. As you will see from the photograph between pages 144 and 145, I've hardly used any fresh material at all. The snowflake shapes are plastic discs thrown out by a display firm and my flowers are made from sugared almonds!

I had some sugared almonds on a dish and somehow they just seemed to form a flower shape. They looked good, so I racked my brain to invent a means of getting a stem of some sort attached to them. I didn't want to glue anything – I may have wanted to eat them later – and I eventually hit upon plastic cooking film. See the instructions below for how to make them. These almonds could be used in a variety of ways. What about a branch of, say, hawthorn or silver birch, all winter bare, with these flowers attached?

I have had for many years a tall cylinder glass Victorian vase, and had never found a use I liked for it. As I wanted to do a frosty-looking arrangement (very appropriate with the snow inches deep outside), I got the snowflake discs and wedged them beautifully in the top of the vase together with a piece of dri-foam covered with cooking foil to take the other parts of the arrangement. The lower arrangement was sticky-taped to the vase, having just covered the dri-foam in cooking foil.

With the outline created by the snowflakes, the arrangement was more than half done. I clustered glass grapes over the cooking foil and introduced some leaf sprays sprayed silver to flow to the sides. Glass bells to welcome in the New Year were a further addition clustered on one side to give balance to the lower arrangement. Pearl and silver sparklers give a delicate tracery effect to the outline, and all that was then needed was the addition of the home-made sugared almond flowers. I made a focal point line of the flowers in the higher arrangement, 5 in all, and put 3 in the lower arrangement with a cluster on the base glass tray.

'Snowflake' discs
Glass grapes
Silver leaf sprays
Glass bells
Pearl and silver sparklers
Sugared almond flowers

'Flowers'
Sugared almonds
Plastic cooking film
Artificial stamens
Wire

1. *Stretch a small piece of plastic cooking film over 5 almonds, leaving enough for a tail, which you then twist to form a stem.*
2. *With silver florist's rose wire make long hair-pin shapes. Trapping the head of the shape under a thumb nail, keeping one hair-pin leg still, twist the other around clockwise, catching the plastic film stem as you wind the wire.*
3. *A cluster of artificial white stamens makes the centre starting point and 5 film-covered almonds are grouped around. Holding both stamens and almonds in one hand bind the lot together with another piece of silver florist's wire. Florist's stem tape is then spiralled down the stem, making a stunning sugared almond flower.*

St Valentine's Day Dinner

Serves 4

Avocado on Dressed Mushrooms with Lime Yoghurt

Strip Fillet Beef Flamed with Brandy and Cream

Carrots with Pernod

Heart-shaped Genoese Cake with Coconut Pink Icing

Chocolate Truffles

By 14 February the winter is becoming a bore and everyone is longing for a ray of sunshine, so why not give a little informal dinner party for 4 or so in the kitchen, as the main course has to be prepared just before eating. It is the kind of party where the starter plates might even be washed up while you are finishing the beef (what lovely guests they are). The heart-shaped genoese sponge captures in no uncertain sense the spirit of the occasion (and apparently a heart-shaped cake is very traditional).

However, there might be just the 2 of you, and so I would tart up the table in the kitchen, dine purely and simply by candlelight, and bung all the dishes in the sink for the next day! There's something rather special about just 2 of you entertaining yourselves for a change. Go to town on the table, the decorations, the dishes, and you might even have the odd cracker left over from Christmas and New Year to pull. Have a couple of balloon glasses of brandy by firelight, and ruin your figures by eating too many chocolate truffles!

Avocado on Dressed Mushrooms with Lime Yoghurt

This is an easy starter, and most of it, except the avocado, can be prepared well in advance if it's well wrapped in clingfilm. See photograph between pages 144 and 145.

Put the marinade ingredients into a small saucepan, bring to the boil and simmer for 10 minutes. Pass through a sieve and then immediately pour over the mushrooms in a serving dish. Leave to get cold and then cover with clingfilm and chill in fridge.

Just before serving, cut the ripe avocados in half from stalk to base with a stainless-steel knife. Remove stone, and with a large silver serving spoon, scoop out each avocado half in one fell swoop. Slice through each half so that the avocado will fan out. Arrange on chilled plate alongside mushrooms (topside up, naturally), and garnish with sprigs of fennel or dill if available, or a large sprig of parsley. Mix together the yoghurt and lime juice and rind, and spoon a little onto each plate.

Serves 4
8-10 oz (225-275 g) mushrooms
2 avocados
butter and oil

Marinade
1/4 pt (150 ml) good oil
1 tbsp mint or white wine vinegar
1/2 pt (300 ml) white wine
2 tsp sugar
4 black peppercorns
pinch of dry English mustard

Yoghurt dressing
1/2 pt (300 ml) natural yoghurt
juice and grated rind of 1 lime

Strip Fillet Beef Flamed with Brandy and Cream

Cut your fillet steak into 4 equal portions and then into about 10 strips per person; you will have 40 small strips of meat. Season with salt and pepper.

Peel and take off the mushroom stalks, which will leave you with about 5 oz (150 g) caps (the stalks and skins can be used in a soup). Dice the caps finely.

Place the double cream in a 2 pt (a generous l) saucepan, and reduce by half gently. When reduced, warm the diced mushrooms through in the cream.

Meanwhile crush the garlic with the sea salt until a smooth paste, and then fry this in the oil along with the finely chopped onions. When these are nice and golden, add the seasoned strips of meat and cook over a high heat for a few minutes and then add the brandy. Pour the mushroom cream sauce over the cooked fillet strips and serve at once with lots of finely chopped parsley.

Quite often this dish is served with cooked rice, but I prefer it with buttery mashed potatoes and carrots.

Serves 4
1 1/2 lb (675 g) fillet steak, trimmed
salt and freshly ground black
  pepper
8 oz (225 g) mushrooms
1/2 pt (300 ml) double cream
2 cloves garlic
pinch of sea salt
2 tbsp olive oil
3 oz (75 g) onions, finely chopped
2 tbsp cooking brandy

Carrots with Pernod

Serves 4
1 lb (450 g) carrots
¾ pt (425 ml) cold water
1 tsp salt
2 oz (50 g) butter
1 dessertsp Pernod

Peel the carrots and slice into approximately ¼in (6mm) thick slices. Put into a pan, cover with the water and add the salt. Bring to the boil, boil for 3 minutes, and then immediately strain and refresh under cold water.

When you wish to serve them, melt the butter in a pan, add the carrots and cook for a couple of minutes to really warm them through. Throw on the Pernod, turn up heat, toss, then serve immediately.

Heart-shaped Genoese Cake with Coconut Pink Icing

Fills 3 heart-shaped tins
measuring 9 × 9 × 1¼in
(22.5 × 22.5 × 3cm)
8 eggs
8 oz (225 g) caster sugar, sieved
8 oz (225 g) plain flour, sieved
4 oz (100-125 g) butter, melted
vanilla essence
jam
cream
icing
desiccated coconut

Put the eggs into the warmed food mixer bowl, and beat on high speed for a good 12-15 minutes before you start to slowly add the sugar. Add this a little at a time, otherwise the light fluffy mixture will be reduced by half! When the sugar has been taken up by the eggs, carefully fold in the sieved plain flour, followed by the melted butter and a little vanilla essence.

Turn the mixture out into the floured and sugared heart-shaped tins. Bake in the pre-heated oven at 350°F (180°C), Gas 4 for 35 minutes. Cool for a while before turning out onto cooling trays.

Sandwich the 3 cakes together with as much jam and cream as you like to make this delicious gâteau, and coat with pink icing. Decorate with toasted desiccated coconut in a strip around the top edges. Have a romantic evening!

Chocolate Truffles

Makes about 20
6 oz (175 g) good dark chocolate, cut into small pieces
2 oz (50 g) unsalted butter, cut into small pieces
½ tsp vanilla essence
2 egg yolks, lightly beaten
4 tbsp cocoa powder

Melt the chocolate and butter together in a double saucepan, stirring from time to time. Remove from the heat and stir in the vanilla essence, then the egg yolks, little by little. If the mixture is sloppy, put it in the fridge, but otherwise form level tablespoons of mixture into balls and roll in the drinking chocolate. Place on a plastic tray, cover with clingfilm, and put in the fridge.

St Valentine's Day Dinner

A wonderfully romantic time for all lovers (although I believe St Valentine was more renowned for his chastity)! Whether you're holding a big swinging bash for all your romantic friends, or having an intimate dinner for 2, it's an ideal occasion for floral decoration. It could be 3 roses in a simple arrangement or 3 dozen (that will shock any lover when he or she gets the bill!), or you could build on the idea in the photograph (between pages 144 and 145). I found these heart shapes when on holiday in the United States; it wasn't anywhere near 14 February, but I bought them anyway (always think ahead, view the decorative possibilities, and buy, collect, save it).

The heart shapes are made of polystyrene and stained red, and are very light. All I had to do was choose a container, fill it with soaked floral foam, then mount the heart shapes on it, with a small garden cane pushed into the pointed end of the heart. You haven't got polystyrene heart shapes from the United States, I can hear you saying, but you can make your own. Cardboard cut to the required size and shape and either painted or bound with red ribbon, will give exactly the same effect. As will a wire ring bent to shape and covered similarly.

I decided that I wanted the traditional 12 red carnations for the arrangement, and I don't think you need any more than that. With the principal feature of the hearts and the champagne, more flowers aren't necessary. The island base sets the scene, covered in red linen and edged in green braid (see page 76 for details on how to make). The flat dish with the foam is set in the middle, and the hearts are placed first at the two required angles. I wanted a strong bold foliage, so I chose camellia foliage. This should always be washed and polished, and I use spray furniture polish, which works very well. I threaded the foliage through the hearts starting at the top and working down to the left-hand side. I then grouped the champagne and glasses at the right-hand side to balance the foliage on the right. A bow of velvet ribbon (see page 145) was then placed towards the front, again giving some weight towards the base. With only a limited number of flowers, you have to be very careful with the placements. Start at the top with the first flower and grade the flowers down towards the centre of the arrangement concentrating 5 flowers in the centre, the focal point. Have 3 main flowers coming forward towards you, which takes the flatness away, and finish off the arrangement with some recessed leaves of the camellia to hide the mechanics of the arrangement.

Whether preparing the arrangement for a huge party or a dinner for 2, keep the red theme going, and with red napkins, green plates, and a glass or two of bubbly, you'll be ready for . . .

Polystyrene heart shapes
Carnations
Camellia foliage
Ribbon bow

Winter Brunch

Serves 6

Muesli

Kidneys in Claret with Mushrooms

Scrambled Eggs with Smoked Salmon and Caviare

Occasionally at a weekend I like to be thoroughly lazy and have a very late breakfast that should really be classed as brunch. I can't yet make up my mind if the Sunday American brunch (and the greatest one is to be found at Café des Artistes on 67th Street at W. Central Park where the menu is mouthwatering) appeals to me so much because of the enormous spicy Bloody Marys one has, or the glasses filled to the brim with Buck's Fizz!

Once again I go to town on the table setting and do everything the day before. The dishes I mention in this meal can be prepared with ease for any number, up to 12, but for me 12 is too many so early in the day. Much better to have 6 at the most. If you greet them with Bloody Marys make them well; sea salt round the rims of the glasses, celery sticks, lime or lemon wedges, Worcestershire sauce, a touch of Tabasco, lots of freshly ground black pepper, and cold, cold, tomato juice instead of ice cubes (which thin it all down too much).

Muesli

Muesli is a firm favourite of mine. It is something which can be boringly bland when you're frugal, but devilishly delicious when you're a trifle extravagant.

Just get a large plastic bowl, make your basic cereal from one or more bases, and then keep on adding all the other ingredients in bibs and bobs. Combine well, store in an airtight container and keep somewhere dry.

For the photograph (opposite page 145) I layered all the ingredients in undulating lines – wheat, barley flakes, sesame seeds, dried banana flakes, fruit, sultanas, coconut, chopped prunes – in a beautiful see-through dish. Guests can help themselves to as little or as much as they wish, using a soup ladle from posh dish or plastic container. Serve with soft brown sugar and top of the milk.

Cereal bases
barley
oats
rye
wheat, whole or cracked

Additions
nuts
dried fruit (sultanas, raisins,
*   currants, prunes, apples,*
*   peaches, pears, apricots)*
desiccated coconut
sesame and poppy seeds
pine kernels
dried banana flakes
fresh fruit, chopped

Kidneys in Claret with Mushrooms

This makes a lovely filling for puff pastry or for the middle of a piped circle of rich mashed potato. It's also good to serve in 3in (7.5cm) ramekins, accompanied by croûtons, or as the filling of a croustade.

Melt the butter in a frying pan and fry the onions until nice and golden. Roughly chop the kidneys and add to pan. Cook for 2 minutes only. Sprinkle on the flour and cook for a further 2 minutes only, stirring. Then pour on the booze, add the mushrooms, and cook for a further 2 minutes only, stirring. Serve at once in ramekins, with a triangular croûton if you like.

Serves 6
4 oz (100-125 g) butter
8 oz (225 g) onions, finely diced
12 oz (350 g) lamb's kidneys,
*   skinned, fibres and core*
*   removed*
1 oz (25 g) flour
¼ pt (150 ml) claret (or good red
*   wine)*
6 oz (175 g) mushroom caps, finely
*   chopped*

Scrambled Eggs with Smoked Salmon and Caviare

Lightly beat the eggs and cream together with a touch of salt and lots of pepper. Melt the oil and butter together in a saucepan, and then pour in all the beaten eggs. With an electric whisk or wire whisk beat until the egg begins to set, and then remove the saucepan immediately from the heat. The pan's heat will continue cooking the eggs while you continue beating. Mix in the cubes of smoked salmon, portion out onto warmed plates, and top with caviare. Serve – and eat – immediately.

Per person
3 eggs
1 tbsp double cream
salt and black pepper
1 tsp oil
1 oz (25 g) butter
2 oz (50 g) smoked salmon, finely
*   diced*
1 tsp American red salmon
*   caviare roe*

Winter Brunch

The pomander tree is an idea that could be considered at any time of year. It could be made colourful and amusing for a children's party; it could have dried or sprayed materials for when natural plant materials are scarce, it can be as luxurious, as colourful, as natural as you want. It is very easy to do, and can be prepared well in advance, and the base lasts for almost ever.

Hammer 4 nails about 2in (5cm) long into a broom handle at right angles to the pole and about 2in (5cm) from one end. Mix some plaster of paris in a bucket, keeping it fairly stiff in texture, and fill a plastic 6in (15cm) plant pot to within an inch (2.5cm) of the top. Let the plaster set a little and then force the un-nailed end of the pole into the centre of the pot. Let this stand until the plaster has completely set, then paint the pole, pot and plaster with matt green paint. When the tree is finished, you can sprinkle some gravel on the top of the plaster of paris to give it a natural effect.

With the stem part finished, prepare the top of the tree. Soak half a block of floral foam thoroughly, then let it drain for a few moments. Cover in plastic film, securing with tape, and push the block onto the broom handle top until it rests against the nails. Now you can cover the block with foliage – use something fairly hardy like box (buxus) – to make a 'clipped ball' shape, rather like the bay trees one sees outside restaurants. You can leave your tree green, but you can also insert flowers to make it look like an indoor tree in blossom. If making the tree for a special occasion, you can prepare it to the foliage stage, cover with a plastic bag, and leave for a couple of days.

When choosing your flowers, go for round-shaped flowers, such as spray carnations, spray chrysanthemums or roses, and cut the stems with a slanting cut so that they can be pushed through the film sheeting into the floral foam. Work all the way around the ball pushing in the flowers in various places to give the all-round effect you want.

The same pomander idea can be adapted for hanging arrangements (without the broom handle, of course), which are useful when space is limited in a room or on the table. Soak a half brick of floral foam, and cover it in plastic film. Wrap it up like a parcel with string coming in from all 4 sides, and finishing with a knotted loop, which can be used as the hanger. A group of 3 hanging pomanders, hung at different levels from ribbons attached to the string loop look most effective.

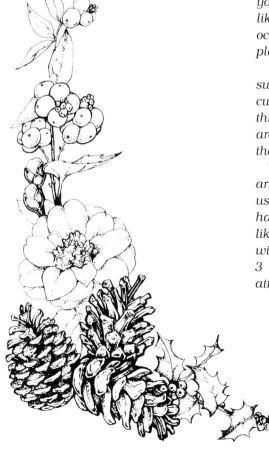

Derek Bridges' Ideas for the Table

Everyone has different ideas about how to decorate their dining tables for parties, whether for sit-down or buffet meals, and so much depends on individual taste, and indeed on the cutlery and china you have. I won't lay down any rules, therefore, but will throw a few ideas on the table, so to speak, and hope they wil inspire you to greater and more adventurous things.

Tablecloths
You either like tablecloths and use them, or you don't bother and use place mats instead. It all depends upon the table, of course: if you're using an old trestle table you'll need a cloth, but if you have a glorious wood or glass table, who would want to hide it? A tablecloth or piece of fabric used as a cloth does, of course, give you a colour scheme for the table setting, but this too can be dictated by the room itself, or the expedient of a place mat.

I don't like white damask; although beautiful material, the dead whiteness can kill any scheme, and I only think it works with a green and white setting. I once did a small demonstration at the local 'pudding school', and went on about how coloured tablecloths can transform a setting. I later discovered from the principal that her girls were taught to use nothing but white damask! Returning a year later, I skirted around the subject of cloths, only to be told that in the intervening months, they'd changed their ideas, and all that damask had been dyed glorious colours!

You can, of course, buy very beautiful tablecloths and matching napkins, but they are expensive, so why not ring the changes by buying lengths of dress material or furnishing fabric. Simple hemming is probably all that's needed, and it will work out very much cheaper as well as adding such variety to your dinner tables. Instead of one cloth that is brought out at every occasion, you can have many at a fraction of the cost. I use a lot of dress material for napkins and cloths; it launders well, the colours don't fade, and the varieties of colours introduced mean that I can use loads of different flower colours every time I entertain.

Boxing and Swagging
Boxing a table for a buffet party is easy and a good idea, as I don't like to see table legs showing under a cloth. If you do a fair amount of party giving it would be sensible to have a piece of hardboard cut to the size of your dining table; this protects the top anyway, and also means you can pin the boxing material into the hardboard and not the table. Obviously I can't say how much fabric you need, but you'll probably want at least 4 times the length of your table, with the width determined by the width of the table.

If the table is going against the wall, position it roughly, and start off by laying the fabric straight across the table from end to end. At one end leave a 2in (5cm) overhanging piece and have all the surplus material at the other end. Pin the overlay onto the underside of the hardboard, and also at various intervals across the back side of the hardboard to hold the fabric in place. Now pick up the surplus fabric, folding it carefully round the corner, and take it round the front of the table to the far corner where you started. Pin the top corner of the fabric to that corner, and work your way across the width, round the front to the back corner where you had all the surplus fabric. With straight dressmakers' pins, pin the skirt part to the top, folding it in, and letting it hang straight. Work the whole way along that top edge, pinning the skirt to the flat top piece of fabric about every 12in (30cm). When you get to the last corner finish with a pin and tuck the surplus under the table.

If your table is going to be central, for your guests to walk all the way around, use more material, and take the surplus fabric right round the table before you start pinning your way back. Again get rid of the surplus material under the table, but bring enough fabric back to seam up with the original straight edge and pin both edges together.

It may seem to be too much trouble to do this with all the pins, but it would take even longer to make a cloth on a sewing machine. And don't forget that when the party is over all you do is unpin and wash one straight piece of fabric; a quick iron and it's ready for the next party!

For the spring wedding picture (opposite page 56) I boxed the table as above, but created some swagging over the top. This is also fairly easy to do if you follow these simple instructions. Once you have boxed your table, take a separate length of fabric, at least 3 times the length of the table. Measure the drop length at the end of the table (usually about 30in or 75cm) and start to pleat the fabric together this length from one end of the fabric. With a florist's reel wire catch the gathered area, twist the wire legs together, and make a small loop at the top. This loop is then drawing-pinned into the hardboard top at the first corner.

Go along the table top edge with the fabric, making as many swags as you like, but too many is too much! Let the fabric fall naturally into a sweep and take it up again into pleating, caught again with a wire. Make a loop at the back and pin again into the hardboard. Keep going across the table front with the sweeps and gathers until you reach the other front corner where your final gather will be and your second falling tail. If you have any surplus fabric I suggest you cut it off neatly.

Where the fabric has been brought up in the sweeps to the top of the table, you can fix bows of ribbon (see page 145) or clusters of fresh or dried flowers.

Napkins and Place Mats

Making your own napkins is easy. Use dress material the same as your tablecloth, or pick out one of the colours if the tablecloth is patterned. I use linen textured material, and from 1 yard (90cm) I make 6 oblong napkins (this venturing away from the traditional square will be explained in a moment). Take each oblong of material, and pull the threads out for about ¹/₂in (1.25cm) on all 4 sides. I don't bother machining along the selvedge because I don't think it's worth the effort, but of course you can, and you could even hem round the edges.

Place mats are made in exactly the same way as the napkins, from the same linen type fabric. Place mats usually are oblong, but I believe in getting the most out of a little: one week I have, say, brown place mats with orange napkins; the brown shapes are pressed flat for the place mats, and the orange shapes are rolled to go into the home-made napkin rings (see page 42). The next time I entertain, if I fancy the same autumnal combination of colours, but used slightly differently, I will use the brown shapes as napkins and the orange shapes as place mats! That is why I don't make napkins square – you can't have square place mats – and your guests aren't going to fuss about oblong napkins!

Place Cards

Place cards can be a very attractive addition to the table. Once again, these must be part of the whole setting. You could simply use a plain card with the guest's name beautifully written on it, with a strip of ribbon to match your colour scheme glued down one side; or you could make a small bow, or group some small dried or silk flowers together with florist's wire and glue them onto the side of the card.

You could cut different shapes out of card, plain or coloured, and tailor them to the occasion. For St Valentine's Day, you could have red heart-shaped cards tucked into the napkin; for Christmas you could have tree-shaped cards. For an Easter party a yellow fluffy chick could hold the card in his beak. For a children's party the ideas must be endless: small sticks of rock with cards attached to each; the little Christmas baskets on page 84 could have a name card tucked inside. Children like their names attached to anything. They could take up a few minutes' worth of party time, searching out their names and places, and they can take the card/present home with them. Similarly the place card could serve two purposes at the same time at Christmas; you could wrap small presents and leave them with the name card on them at each guest's place.

These are just a few ideas to start you thinking – I'm sure you will come up with many more of your own.

Index